The Global Adventurer's Handbook

by John Malarkey

PERPETUAL
P R E S S

Seattle, Washington

Printed in Canada

First edition

10 9 8 7 6 5 4 3 2 1

Cover: Allegro Design

Interior: Greeneye Design

Publisher's note: The purpose of *The Global Adventurer's Handbook* is to help light the way with insider tips and ideas for better self-led adventure traveling. This book is designed to give you the most objective information possible, based on experiences of travel veterans and industry research. While we have made every attempt to provide up-to-date details and accurate prices, these can change abruptly. To ensure a superior adventure, be sure to double-check all information before making final decisions and embarking on your travels.

Library of Congress Card Catalog Number: 94-074012.

ISBN 1-881199-40-1

Table of Contents

Acknowledgments

This book came about due to the efforts of a lot of great people. I'd especially like to thank the staff at Perpetual Press who continue to make each step of the journey possible. Jennifer DuBois did a fine job supervising the editing, lassoing wild prose into cogent points.

If it weren't for the love and contributions of my fellow life traveler and wife Kerry Milne, this book would be just a dream. It's hers, too.

I'd also like to thank Geoffrey Moore for advice; Dominican Sister Susannah Malarkey for insight; Len Stevens for sound counsel; Jim Joiner for inspiration; and literary agent Arielle Eckstut of James Levine Communications, for guidance.

This book is dedicated to all the people I've met traveling who have invited me into their worlds: I'm grateful. And, to my Mother and Father, who gave me my first passport and showed me the road to adventure.

Additional credits and thanks:

Interior photos: pp. 9, 31: Joseph A. Losi; pp.40, 82, 101,107, 138: Richard Kleebaur; pp. 18, 63: Kerry Milne; pp. 74, 124,132: Gilbert Meigs; pp. 16, 24 , 52, 79: Deirdre Malarkey.

For sharing personal travel experiences: the staffs of Perpetual Press, Clarke Canfield, Gordon Malarkey, Peter Malarkey, Andrea Linsky, Deb Eder, Jinx Faulkner, Paul Koehler, Tom Koehler, Neil Koehler, Bruce McNamer, James Meigs, Marybeth Crowe, Lisa Moore, Joe & Rhonda Rosenbaum, Horst & Ute Homar, Art & Ruby Milne, Monica Klinkam, Greg Stewart, John Iammatteo, Tom Turnell, Jay & Kathleen Goodfriend, Tim Reilly, Don & June Farries, Karline Bird, Jim & Sandy Smith, Marc Kittner & Jane Faulkner, John & Nan Gallagher, Gilbert & Laurie Meigs and Family, Mary B. Malarkey, and many others.

Introduction 1

There are thousands of uninhabited tropical islands around the globe you can boat to and live on, undiscovered, for as long as you want.

▲▼▲▼▲▼▲▼▲▼▲▼▲▼▲▼▲▼▲▼▲▼▲▼▲

You can ride a hot air balloon over Serengeti National Park, in Africa, and glide silently over giraffe, zebras and lions.

▲▼▲▼▲▼▲▼▲▼▲▼▲▼▲▼▲▼▲▼▲▼▲▼▲

White explorer Richard Burton in the 1800s learned Arabic, darkened his skin, and walked across hostile Saudi Arabia to Mecca disguised as a Bedouin. He succeeded.

Imagine...sitting on an ancient ridge in Scotland at dawn, watching the sunrise transform a dark and misty valley into the world's largest glistening emerald.

...Digging into spicy fare at a colorful Arab bazaar, and listening to robed merchants banter in a strange tongue.

...Hopping over a fallen coconut and feeling the scrunch of sugary white sand between your toes on a tropical beach in Thailand.

Thoughts of Travel

Are you an adventurer, or do you want to be? Is something pulling you away that you can't describe? Do you feel like bursting out to roam exotic places, but you don't want to spend a lot of money or go on a big group tour? You're not alone. If you're ready to set out to explore the world cheaply and independently, read on.

This book isn't about one- or two-week vacations, escorted tours, or great-but-costly adventures lasting seventeen days. It's about major, extended foreign exploring. It's about taking the time to really escape—to enjoy long, exotic trips, instead of short ones. In other words, this book is about independent foreign *adventuring* on trips from one to three months, from five to six months, to a year, or even more.

It's about doing it yourself easily and inexpensively.

This get-ready guide explains how to get started with your research, then how to actually get to those foreign places off the beaten path. It equips you to confidently venture into hidden locations, see amazing sights, mingle with diverse people, and enjoy exciting travel experiences most people only dream about. It's a how-to on what many believe is the most enriching and at the same time the most affordable way to travel.

Reading this book will help you prepare to be a traveler abroad—not just another tourist. There is an important distinction between the two. Travelers earn respect, and quite often end up on the receiving end of remarkable, exciting, previously unseen opportunities. Tourists, on the other hand, see only the well-known sites and mostly just get tolerated.

If you won't be satisfied with another "here it is—there it went"

Traveling in far off places brings adventure, discovery, new friends, and fun. Anyone can do it. Annapurna base camp, Nepal.

vacation, and you want to take the time to really explore a part or parts of the world, you've come to the right book. Reading it can help you gain the courage to make that leap. If you already have a trip planned—or you're a veteran traveler—this book can help ensure your next trip's the best ever.

This book examines:

- How long to go

- How to travel with your spouse, a friend, by yourself, or with your family

- What to take with you and what to leave behind

- How much to pay for your trip, and how to pay only what you need, when you need

- How to finance pay-as-you-go trips by working en route
- How to sift through travel advice before and during your trip
- What to expect when you arrive, and throughout your journey
- How to decide whether traveling is right for you at this point in your life
- How to overcome the resistance of yourself and others to such a trip
- Coming home

...and much more.

Whether you're seventeen or seventy, this book is about taking matters into your own hands. There's actually as much to unlearn about taking an affordable alternative adventure trip as there is to learn. For example, you might expect to pay a king's ransom for this kind of adventure, right? Wrong. With ease you can live in foreign countries cheaply. That is, travel about, eat well, and stay in clean, comfortable accommodations for as little as $500–$700 per month.

Much of the preparing and going process may be new and slightly bewildering, but the rewards are infinite.

There's true adventure waiting—fun, mind-enriching encounters—and personal growth. Do it right and you'll return with great photos, videos, tape recordings, and journals. You'll bring back beautiful art, clothing, jewelry and other handmade crafts, incredible memories, and new friends and contacts from wherever you go. You will have seen exotic people living in ways utterly different than yours. And if you're like most people, you'll come home a happier human being.

Here's a great passage on getting up and going:

Until one is committed, there is hesitancy, the chance to draw back, always ineffectiveness.

Concerning all acts of initiative (and creation), there is one elementary truth (the ignorance of which kills countless ideas and splendid plans). That is the moment one definitely commits oneself, then Providence moves, too.

All sorts of things occur to help one that would never have otherwise occurred. A whole stream of events issues from the decision, raising in one's

favor all manner of unforeseen incidents and meeting and material assis-
tance which no person could have dreamed would have come his way.

Whatever you can do, or dream you can, begin it. Boldness has genius,
power and magic to it. Begin it now.

—Johann Goethe (1749–1832)

Call To Adventure 2

Italian monks, departing from China in the 1300s, hid silkworms in their walking staffs, thus bringing the secret behind silk to the West.

▲▼▲▼▲▼▲▼▲▼▲▼▲▼▲▼▲▼▲▼▲▼▲▼▲

If you see a brightly colored frog in the tropics, don't touch. Some have toxic skin.

▲▼▲▼▲▼▲▼▲▼▲▼▲▼▲▼▲▼▲▼▲▼▲▼▲

Travel to Southern France and you can still see standing Roman aquaducts that brought water from the Alps, 200 miles away.

Picture these moments: the luscious scent of jasmine lulling you to sleep, then later, the hoots of jungle gibbons at dawn, stirring you from tropical slumber. The reassuring warmth of a cup of hot green tea in your cold hands as you gaze at slashes of gold sunset on the Himalayas. Floating on a bamboo river raft until it falls apart, then leaping ashore...These images may sound a little far out. But you don't have to be far out to consider them. In today's world, it's easy to make them come true. In fact, the only crazy part is to deny yourself the opportunity.

Eyes on the Horizon

Considering a Break

There's only one thing to do if you feel it's time to take off. Go! Many people feel the worldly wanderlust all the time, and do nothing about it. Others feel this way quite often, and honor it. It's easier to do than people think. It can change your life. It also can require you to rearrange your life in order to pull it off.

Whether you're single, married, working, retired, a student, financially secure or just squeaking by, a home owner, or a parent, you can do it. I've done it and so has Kerry, my wife. On our most recent off-beat adventure, we saved up our money, left our jobs, and traveled for seven months through the South Pacific and Southeast Asia. Then we came home and eventually found jobs in our respective fields once again.

Types of Travel

Before we were married, we each had traveled around parts of Europe and the Middle East at various times for three weeks to four months per trip. All our excursions consisted of "first generation" and "second generation" travel.

First generation travel is what's known as the top-hat approach, harkening back to high-style travel in nineteenth-century Europe: lots of luggage, a comfy hotel, and familiar Western food. It's based on the idea of maintaining the comforts (and isolations) of home life while away, and really is just plain old straight-ahead tourism.

Second generation travel is modern discovery travel, or the straw-hat approach to immersion in the culture you're visiting. It's trying to speak a few words of the local language, learning the local gestures and social customs, traveling the local way via trains or buses or pedicabs or oxcart or canoe, and visiting markets, local festivals, and art centers. It's dumping your opinions, accepting the charms and habits of the local people, and keeping an open mind. It's non-exploitive, exploratory, respectful, and low-impact.

Third-generation travel is genuine guerrilla travel. It's beyond the focus of this book, and is suited only for the truly intrepid. It's going native, the hornbill-feathers-stuck-in-your-hair approach. Here, the package tour visitor evolves through the progressive traveler model to become primitive. It's the partial or sometimes total abandonment of twentieth-century life through traveling and living with indigenous peoples for lengthy periods. This appeals to very hardy, experienced travelers, and if you're game, it's out there.

> In a country campground near Adelaide, Australia, we fell asleep once to the wind softly rustling the eucalyptus trees. We woke with a start in the morning to roaring lions. Lions in Australia? A traveling circus had set up overnight, a hundred yards away.

Nowadays the three categories are beginning to blur. For example, you can have a third-generation trip in a Western, First World nation, like among the Inuit people of northern Canada. Or—thanks to the international hotel business—you can go to a Third World island lost in the 1700s and have a glamorous, modern, first generation stay. For simplicity, this book focuses on the middle ground: self-led second generation travel. Another way to describe it is off-the-beaten-path travel, with a mix of soft and hard adventures.

The New Eco-Tourism

Many people's introduction to second generation travel comes via the eco-tour, a short, expensive, experience-rich version of the off-beat exploration this book is about. A fringe trend that's fast becoming a mainstream travel option in the 1990s, eco-touring takes you where larger commercial package trips don't. They include guided "adventure

Dreamers of all ages feel the adventuring bug. This traveler's about to get the inside on yurt life. Near Ulan Bator, Mongolia.

vacations," "volunteer vacations," "green vacations," "environmental study tours," and so forth. You can count turtles in Costa Rica, hike and look for rare cats in Siberia, paddle the Amazon, or go photo-touring in a Chilean mountain reserve.

Eco-touring is a great way for people to quickly get under the skin of an exotic place or culture, then get home just as efficiently. The best eco-tours offer you global appreciation through intense, local, low-impact participation. And they're a great dress rehearsal for independent adventuring.

Properly spent, a three-week eco-tour fee plus airfare can buy you three to four months of the same kind of travel those tours try to condense into a short period. There's just one key difference: you must guide yourself.

Initial Resistance

You may be thinking that foreign adventuring or second generation travel sounds risky, like taking an untethered spacewalk. When I first started this kind of travel I was skeptical and had to be convinced. But once I was underway, and getting more excited each day that I actually was pulling it off, I was surprised to see how easy it was. Furthermore, I began to meet others who were dwarfing my supposed gargantuan chance-taking. Check out these folks who have made our trips seem like Sunday drives:

Consider the California couple in their mid-twenties we met in Fiji who are spending five years bicycling their way around the globe. Or the Swedish pair in their thirties who sailed halfway around the world to New Zealand over three years. They then sold their boat—a worm-eaten hulk they'd spent eight years rebuilding before the trip (talk about planning!)— then went backpacking through Asia for another year on their way home.

And some people, well, they decide not to come home at all. One young San Francisco woman we know went trekking in Nepal and Thailand, and then instead of returning to the U.S. found a neat job in Hong Kong.

Another friend from Montana, age twenty-six, left his job at an Asian branch of a New York bank (he'd been transferred from San Francisco) to travel in Indonesia. Then he headed to China, met up with his mother, and toured parts of India. During this year of travel his application to the Peace Corps came through and now he's off to Paraguay.

We met a retired Norwegian fellow, sixty-eight years old, who was backpacking in the South Pacific on his way to an assignment in Australia with an international service organization for retired executives.

A middle-aged Kenyan couple and their two children watched a colorful, hypnotic temple dance in Bali, Indonesia with us one evening. This family was traveling together for ten months all over Asia.

An American couple in their fifties bought a Volkswagen van in Europe and drove it east to Burma, then shipped it and themselves through Southeast Asia and all the way to Canada.

Then there's the West German couple in their late twenties we met hiking in New

> No matter where you go... While touring distant Russia, a friend's Mom got to chatting with another traveler. It turns out he was vacationing from Holland, where Mom has an uncle. It further turns out he was from the same town as—and a best friend of—Mom's uncle.

Island-hopping, local style. These travelers are being rowed to an old-style ferryboat for the channel crossing. Taveuni Island, Fiji.

Zealand, who are just working and traveling their way around the world for several years until they find the right place to settle down.

Anything's possible. But first let's concentrate on exploring.

Actively Considering Travel

Reviewing Priorities

In the process of growing up, reality muscles its way into our childhood fantasies of far-off kingdoms and exotic, mysterious people. There's no denying that the societal urge to conform and the financial realities of living in our age threaten the desire to be independent and to explore. But if we keep deferring those travel dreams, and denying the urge to break away, those dreams stay bottled up.

Building Support

The great thing is that adults, with just a little disposable income, can finally achieve the big-time adventure travel they've always wondered about. What holds many of us back is fear. We face the practical counsel of others against such wild travel adventures. ("It's loony." "You won't find a job." "You'll lose your progress in your career." "Frankly, it's just not practical.") Countless experienced travelers would disagree, saying that the great times you have in other lands with other people enrich what you do at home. Overcoming the resistance others put up is easy if you understand that it's partly their own fears being dumped on you.

Examining Benefits

There's personal growth to consider when deciding to take a trip. An excellent approach is to look at adventurous travel as life development. You get to see the world as it is and tear down myths and misconceptions. You learn to get through the unknown, to find answers, to know the joy of discovery, which all contribute to maturity and life experience. You see the history you've read about, and expand your knowledge of world events, cultural behavior, and societal trends. This boosts confidence, tolerance, and the ability to relate to others.

There also are the financial fears involved in travel. One fear may be simply that you can't afford to go. Another stems from the monetary measurement that society applies to being successful, which serves to highlight the money you'll lose by going. The financial concern also is valid for those who are at a great place in their careers and don't want to take a break.

Financially, travel is not a money-making enterprise, but you can make money or at least recoup your expenses through writing, photography, importing, or business contacts made on your travels. Becoming familiar with foreign cultures, languages, and political systems also can give you a leg up in the local and international market.

But for many, the sheer fun of adventure travel defies any price tag.

Tapping Self-Confidence

More deeply, many people's reluctance to leave the known stems from a primal need to feel secure. One way around this instinct is to recognize that those fears crop up due to lack of experience. Like the kid who tiptoes out and hesitantly jumps off a highdive—and then laughingly bursts out of the water and races up the ladder again—a great trip instills in us the knowledge that we can do it again.

Naturally, commitments made before you bought this book might make travel more difficult. You might own a business. Have a payroll to meet. Have children. Be at an important point in your work career. Own properties. But if you've come this far, and keep on reading, you'll get around those obstacles and make extended travel a pursuit you can repeat throughout your life.

Taking The First Steps To Adventure

3

In Java, people tie hooks to kites, and then "fish" for fruit bats that fly over at sunset.

▲▽▲▽▲▽▲▽▲▽▲▽▲▽▲▽▲▽▲▽▲▽▲▽▲

The Great Wall of China, handbuilt of huge stones with a road on top, snakes up hills and down valleys in various stages of disrepair for over 2,000 miles.

▲▽▲▽▲▽▲▽▲▽▲▽▲▽▲▽▲▽▲▽▲▽▲▽▲

Mountain yogis in India walk in the snow barefoot, wear simple loincoths, and don't eat much besides vegetables, rice, and tea boiled from glacier water.

Step One, take a deep breath. Step Two, smile. You're on to something. In this section you'll find suggestions on where to start looking for travel advice, and what to look for. You'll also find tips you can use for planning your departure on this mysterious adventure, whether you're going with friends or family. You're gaining momentum toward leaving on a foreign escape. It's exciting, and it energizes everything you do. Like a track star walking up to the starting block, you're about to burst free.

Examining the Possibility

Unusual Places

So what is "off the beaten path?"

To many, beaten is Los Angeles, Paris, London, Rome, Taipei, Rio, Singapore, Cairo, Tokyo, Moscow, and hundreds of other cities. They're awesome places, with lots of fascination and unique histories. But what if you find yourself wanting to range elsewhere?

An adventurer wants out. An adventurer want to get away from the comforts of standard tourism and Western ways, away from highways and skyscrapers and elevators and TV and fashion and fast food, and into the places that vibrate with "localness"—that simple something that's new, exotic, mysterious, undiscovered, ancient.

Moreover, most experienced travelers would agree that along with sights, there is nothing more fascinating and more rewarding than meeting someone completely unlike yourself. Someone with whom you can exchange a few words in the local language, share a meal, and talk about family, music, art, or ideas. Along with seeing far-away locations, it's this personal contact with people and cultures that makes exploring foreign places endlessly enriching. The closer you stay to home, the more difficult it is to make those contacts.

You'll find the familiar in Western nations and in Westernized pockets of out-of-the-way places. This makes it tougher to have new, exciting experiences.

So where can you go for completely unfamiliar encounters? Get yourself out and about to the little-visited parts of Western Europe,

Central and South America, and to huge, mysterious regions like Africa or Asia. Go to the republics of Eastern Europe, or to the Near and Middle East, or to the many thousands of tropical islands of the vast Pacific. People just like you are doing it this minute. They're experiencing people, places, and cultures completely new to them, and returning home amazed.

Previewing Destinations

Starting the Inquiry

The world offers a lifetime of adventurous travel destinations, and that's why choosing where to go can be agonizing.

Getting to the more remote, exotic places on the globe starts with determining how much time you'll dedicate to the trip. Two months? Five months? A year? More? For planning purposes it's best to decide on a finite length of time. You can always modify it once underway.

Deep down you may have a yearning to get to the beaches of Thailand, or the high reaches of Nepal, or the vast baked landscape of Australia, or the grassy plains of Kenya. You could buy an around-the-globe air ticket that lets you stop in Kathmandu, Bangkok, Sydney, and Nairobi, and actually see all those nations in one trip. Or you could spend your budget and explore just one country up close for a year. How about Brazil? Turkey? The Philippines? The point is that there are as many types and lengths of trips as there are places to go.

Because of the plethora of choices you may be tempted to venture down the path of least resistance. That is, to let others decide for you and go to that month's trendy vacation spot, or perhaps to a place you feel you're expected to visit. Don't. Hold off on making a decision and keep looking.

Sample Trips

To demonstrate short, medium, and long trips here are three examples. Each is based on a real-life scenario and might help you begin to make your own plan.

Short Trip Example: One Month

Rick and Christine Brinson, ages twenty-nine and twenty-eight, from Missoula, Montana, decide to take their first adventure trip, a one-month beach and snorkeling trek to the tropics. Rick's been to Mexico for

Witnessing for one's self the legacy of ancient cultures makes an off-beat trip worth the effort. Petra, Jordan.

Christmas once, but Christine hasn't been outside the U.S. except on their five-day Caribbean honeymoon cruise. After a bit of talking around they hear Hawaii is fairly touristed and expensive. Also, they're interested in unusual peoples. They decide on Fiji, in the South Pacific. It has great reefs, beautiful beaches, warm people with a still-intact native culture, and is less expensive than Tahiti. Also, there are regular flights from the west coast.

They begin planning their trip six months before leaving, and dutifully save money, clip coupons, and skip major purchases. Upon leaving, both take two weeks off from work and arrange to take two additional unpaid weeks off. They stay the first week in a hotel reserved beforehand, then shift to a beach bungalow resort, meeting fun couples from Australia, Sweden, and elsewhere. They alternate eating out with kitchen-made meals. In short, they have a blast.

Medium Trip Example: Five Months

Candace Wong, age twenty-one, from Philadelphia, decides to take her junior year off from college. She wants to travel somewhere far away. Her friend and housemate Laurie agrees to go, too. But both need to save money. At the end of her sophomore year, Candace works full-time as a waitress from July through March and Laurie gets a job on a landscape crew. Candace came to the U.S. from China with her family when she was two. She's been to see relatives in Vancouver, Canada, and Paris for a week each, and visited China once while in high school.

A month before leaving, Laurie breaks her leg skiing and cancels.

No matter. Candace's older brother is a U.S. Navy officer in Italy. Candace has saved enough for a five-month trip, gives notice at her job, and hops a plane to Italy. She stays three weeks there, then spends four adventurous months traveling around Turkey, Greece, North Africa, and the Mediterranean. She hooks up with other single travelers, and makes many friends.

In August, Candace returns from her five months off in time to re-enter college for her junior year.

Longer Trip Example: One Year

Horace and Althea Baker, in their late forties, from Savannah, Georgia, decide to take a year-long vacation. Horace works as a school district administrator, and Althea works as a paralegal. Their twin daughters are in college. Horace has always wanted to go back to Asia since being stationed in Vietnam during the conflict there. Althea wants to see something of Africa after experiencing that culture in the Caribbean and Rio on several earlier beach vacations.

They decide to do both. They start saving nine months ahead of time, figuring they'll be in Third World locations and will have about a third of a normal year's expenses. Horace proposes an unpaid leave of absence and gets it. Althea quits her job, figuring she'll easily get another, as paralegals are in demand.

Their first two months of the trip will be paid for by accumulated vacation time at both their jobs. More comes from their savings and Horace's 401k plan, which allows for loans. The daughters already pay for most of school with scholarships, loans, and work. The Bakers find a tenant for their home and assign a property manager, and Althea's sister is given the power of attorney in all matters.

Horace and Althea meet another couple at a slide show before going to Africa, and spend the first month of their trip with them in Kenya. Then they visit Tanzania, Zimbabwe, the Seychelles, and Madagascar. The second half takes them through Southeast Asia, landing in Bangkok and touring Thailand, Vietnam, Cambodia, Malaysia, and Indonesia.

They have the time of their lives.

Gathering Ideas

Globes and Atlases

To get ideas on where to go, take a really good look at a globe and store the shapes and locations of the continents in your head. You'll continually refer to this mental image while you're planning. Look at a good world atlas to examine the planet a little more closely. In combination with these previews, take that all-important first pilgrimage: visit a travel bookstore.

Travel Bookstores and Libraries

Standing in a bookshop travel section and staring at all the well-designed, attractively photographed travel guidebooks can be confusing. You'll either be mesmerized by the possibilities or frustrated by the lack of time you have, or both. Give yourself some time to take in all the material. Begin by thumbing through the books that look interesting, then start focusing on the part of the world that appeals to you. Also, visit a library and roam the card catalogs, microfiche, or computer databases for destination ideas.

Travel Agents

You may be able to locate a travel agency that caters to budget travelers to help plan your trip. Nationally, Council Travel, a division of the New York-based Council on International Educational Exchange (CIEE), is good. Also try the Student Travel Association (STA), the international travel agency based in Sydney, Australia. Both are located in larger cities around the U.S., and have a college student focus but welcome all ages.

There are many other travel agents that concentrate on budget travel. Check your local newspaper's travel section or the phone book.

Because more people these days are heading out on short-term, all-inclusive adventure package tours, mainstream travel agents are getting better acquainted with the nitty-gritty details of off-beat locations. You may have good luck with them. But because travel agents work for a commission you must make sure their advice fits your plans. To double-check on an agent's services ask for the name of a client who bought tickets for a trip similar to the self-led adventure you're planning, and ask them how satisfied they were with the service.

Friends

It's a perfect time to begin asking around to friends who've traveled. Or ask if anybody knows of anyone who's done it. Talk to them. Have them show you pictures, and get their advice. Don't worry if you have more questions than books or people can answer. Your trip itself will fill in the remaining blanks.

Hot Off-Beat Travel Spots
'89 Kenya, Tanzania
'90 China
'91 Thailand
'92 Costa Rica, Belize
'93 Eastern Europe
'94 Vietnam
'95 South America
'96 Central Asia

Sports Stores

Many sports equipment stores, outfitters, and travel bookstores show slideshows of adventure trips. An early outfitter, Abercrombie & Fitch out of San Francisco, provided Teddy Roosevelt with a heavy chainmail suit to deflect arrows in the Amazon. Fortunately, today's travel purveyors focus on lighter gear and information to match today's needs.

Newspapers and Magazines

University daily newspapers are a great place to look for travel events. As for urban or suburban newspapers, they stay mostly topical. Occasionally there's an in-depth article or nuggets of information useful to the foreign explorer, but not often. Glossy travel magazines tend to be geared toward high-end shoppers. So you have to ferret out information from travelers' newsletters or magazines like *EcoTraveler*, *National Geographic Traveler*, *Escape*, or *Outside* to get a more in-depth view. Look in the back, too, for brochures from travel arms of foreign governments.

The magazines of conservation organizations highlight areas that may interest you. These might include magazines from the Sierra Club, The Nature Conservancy, The National Audubon Society, and others. And of course, don't overlook the fine standard-bearer: the National Geographic Society.

TV and Movies

Watch public TV and cable stations for shows and documentaries dealing with what's really happening at the local level around the world. Rent or see documentaries and foreign-language films. The larger video stores have travel sections where you can get visual overviews of specific destinations as well as whole countries.

Focusing on Specific Destinations

Adventure Vacation Brochures

An excellent way to see color photos and get descriptions of current conditions of exotic areas is to send for adventure travel brochures. In the back of any travel magazine are ads and toll-free telephone numbers of larger outfits like Mountain Travel, International Expeditions, and other adventure travel companies that cater to the short-term adventure traveler.

Flipping through catalogues will give you excellent ideas on what appeals to you. Gorillas, gazelles, and elephants? Snowcapped peaks and mountain valleys? Colorful parrots floating through green rainforests? Sun-drenched, white sand beaches melting into azure lagoons? Exotic handicrafts in Moroccan bazaars? These catalogues give you a chance to point and say "yes—that's where I want to go." You may decide to go on a trip with one of these firms in order to get your feet wet as a precursor to a future longer trip. Or, the colorful pages may inspire you to do it on your own now.

Hands-On Guidebooks

Beyond talking to someone who's been somewhere and seeing their pictures, detailed travel handbooks offer a great way to preview an area. They help you pick destinations because they're written in a factual style, with straight-ahead photography. This real-life approach also can clear away your illusions, possibly prompting you to go elsewhere. These books help avoid the disappointment that can be brought on by overly lush descriptions.

Start with specific area guidebooks written by and for the independent budget traveler. For area descriptions, prices, lodging, transportation, cultural, and artistic background, try the Lonely Planet Publications' *Travel Survival Kit* series (and their "Updates," a series of recent letters from travelers), Moon Publications' Travel Handbook guides; The *Rough Guides*, the *Berkeley Guides*, the Harvard Press *Let's Go* series, *Passport Guides*, and the Apa *Insight* guides. All these have a reputation for being reliable and accurate. For comparison purposes, nose into any other books that happen to cover the area that interests you, such as the John Muir Publications "Back Door" series and the Fodor's or Frommer's budget travel guides. More are being created every year, but the above guides have long been dedicated to the low-cost, high cultural value kind of trip we're discussing.

If you're flying, training, or bussing to your destination, you can save money by buying travel guides only for the first few countries you'll be visiting. By all means read up on the other countries in your itinerary. But if you're going on a long trip of several months or more, don't walk out of a bookshop loaded down with guides you won't use until later. Overseas bookshops sell used (and thus cheaper) copies of these same guidebooks, exchanged by travelers who've already seen those countries.

Explorer Accounts and Early Travel Literature

Personal travelogues and explorer journals from history offer fascinating portrayals of certain regions. If you can't find any in your library, you might end up writing your own.

Accounts of early exploration abound. These life-is-stranger-than-fiction chronicles can whet your appetite for an area, and serve as a window to the way things were. They also can give you a history of the region, which can help you better understand the culture. A few of the many examples include books recounting the travels of Marco Polo, Alfred Russel Wallace, Henry Stanley, David Livingstone, Mark Twain, Charles Doughty, Mary Kingsley, Margaret Mead, and many more. These are listed under Travel Literature in bookstore sections, or by subject in libraries. Fiction also can be enjoyable, such as James Clavell's Noble House series about Hong Kong. Just remember that fiction is entertainment, not necessarily an accurate portrayal of what you'll find in the world.

Modern Travel Literature

Good, modern, non-fiction travel writing has turned many an armchair traveler into a bona fide plane-hopper. A few of the better ones are listed below:

- *Ring of Fire* by Lorne and Lawrence Blair
- *Arabian Sands* by Wilfred Thesiger
- *The Happy Isles of Oceania* by Paul Theroux
- *Journey to Russia* by Laurens van der Post
- *Out Of Africa* by Isak Dinesen
- *Video Night in Kathmandu* by Pico Iyer
- *Arabia through the Looking Glass* by Jonathan Raban
- *The Fearsome Void* by Geoffrey Moorhouse

- *Eastern Approaches* by Fitzroy MacLean
- *The Snow Leopard* by Peter Mathiessen
- *Among The Believers* by V.S. Naipaul
- *Arctic Dreams* by Barry Lopez
- *Running the Amazon* by Joe Kane
- *The Songlines* by Bruce Chatwin
- *Stranger In The Forest* by Eric Hansen

This represents a fraction of what's good and readily available. I've found it's fun to read a traveler's tale about a place while you're actually in the place yourself, so you can compare reflections.

Maps

A good map shop will have up-to-date international maps for focusing more specifically on the places you'll be heading. If you're flying to a country, most guidebooks you'll buy before leaving will include area maps and city maps, so you won't need a big national map. Combined with local maps purchased in-country, you'll do just fine.

It's a different story if you bike, hike, hitchhike, drive, or sail to your destination and onward. If so, you'll obviously want the best maps you can get before you leave, because you'll be relying on them to help you find your way. Your best bet if traveling overland is to get country maps before leaving. Once in a country you'll still have good luck finding maps, although they may not be current or as detailed as you'd like, especially in Asia. Various travel and camping organizations around the world have roadmaps and campground guides similar to those offered by the American Automobile Association (AAA) and Kampgrounds Of America (KOA) in the U.S. You also can call or write a country's U.S. embassy or its tourism office in Washington, D.C.

Sifting through Your Information

Facts Review

You'll be inundated with information about your trip, but it's important to take plenty of time to absorb it all. Then, once you've put good time into deciding where you'd like to go, things may get topsy-turvy for awhile. Feel free to change your mind. Our last time out we dreamed of going to colonial East Africa, crashing through the brush of the African

Much awaits the traveler curious about the spiritual side of culture. *Goddess Ulu Danu Temple, Bedugul, Bali, Indonesia.*

veldt on photo safari with tents, wild animals, porters, and everything khaki! We bought the books, got the brochures. But after gathering information and talking to people, we did a 180-degree turn. We ended up doing seven months of Southeast Asian temples, beaches, and snorkeling in thongs and tank tops.

Just start following the trickle of an idea to the big river of actually going, even if you change directions along the way. Exactly where you want to explore will finally emerge.

Seasons and Temperature

Another factor to consider is time of year. Ignore what the weather's like where you live and focus on what's going on where you're headed. You don't want to go to India during monsoon season, or to the tropics during hurricane season, or to Inner Mongolia in winter.

When planning a trip a lot of people forget that while the structure of twenty-four hour time is the same everywhere you go, seasons aren't. So here's a quick geography review to help your thinking.

The world is a sphere split by the equator into two equal hemispheres, the northern and southern. Navigators chart points on the globe using a system of latitude and longitude. Due to a still-prevailing Eurocentric view of cartography, longitude measures distance east or west of Greenwich, England, and is represented on a map by vertical lines. Latitude measures distance north or south of the equator and is shown with horizontal lines.

For the first step in calculating weather, think in simple colors. Imagine that the polar areas are always white (cold). The equatorial areas are always red (hot). But the in-between zones—the temperate latitudes— alternate (between (pink) and chilly (blue-green) because the earth is tilted to one side. As it orbits the sun over a year, the sun travels across the sky from winter to summer, then back again. When the north temperate latitudes are warm the south temperate latitudes are chilly.

For example, when it's winter in Colorado, it's balmy summer in New Zealand.

Now the next factor: altitude. Want to sun and snorkel in the Caribbean, or hike and mountain camp in the Andean cordillera? You can do both all year long. But how, you might ask, they're both on the same latitude and the same longitude and in the same time zone? The difference is altitude. One is at sea level and is always warm and sunny. The other is at a high elevation and typically frosty. Saying it's December is irrelevant in the Caribbean except that it signifies the tourist season. It's always summer there. And in the high elevations of South America, it's always brisk, even in August.

So forget "Christmas means snow" and "July Fourth means barbecue weather." When planning your trip think in terms of cold versus warm and wet versus dry.

The more you read, the more you'll begin to fit your trip into the weather patterns. This is critical if you hope to enjoy your experience to the fullest. If by chance your adventure takes you to warm *and* cold zones, you still can adapt. The colder destinations around the globe call for more gear, so your luggage in cold places will be heavier. You can pack for both climates before you leave, then depart with just one set of clothes. Then when you shift to the other climate type, you can ship home the gear you no longer need and make arrangements for the second batch to arrive in its place.

> **If it looks like the 747 jumbo next to you on the runway has creatures staring out the windows, it does. Shippers use converted jets to fly sheep, goats, horses, fish, and other livestock to and from world locations for breeding, farming, and to meet "flown in fresh" demand.**

Personal Considerations

Spiritual and Religious

Because travel is often as much an inward journey as an outward one, you may not have practical reasons for traveling at this time in your life. That you simply want to go is reason enough.

While you're researching for tangible places to visit there also may be an internal groping that doesn't have its destination readily defined by border markings on a globe. The desire to embark on this kind of spiritual quest may be being prompted within the context of a belief you follow. For example, it could be photographs on the wall of your Baptist church showing the appealing faces of other Baptist folks in some far-off land.

Alternatively, you may wish to compare what you know against something you feel is out there that you haven't discovered yet. Or you may want to put aside your family religion and explore something new. Everything you're feeling about traveling is valid.

Any *National Geographic* magazine will remind you that there are as many religious beliefs and practices—or ways to understanding our-selves—as there are tribes of people on the globe. Many regions of the world are filled with people for whom religion and daily life are one and the same. Spend time among these people and you may soon feel quite comfortable with their practices.

In our travels, spiritually focused people in the Middle East, Fiji, Mexico, Thailand, and parts of Indonesia have affected us greatly. Encounters have made us less wishful for material things, and instead given us more simple ways to be fulfilled. And we've developed a respect and appreciation for diversity.

For some people, experiencing an entirely new culture makes the quest a success. They may come home changed. They may come home neutral. Or, they may hightail it home to a religion they know, suddenly ready to get into it like never before. Regardless, they return a richer person. All the gold in the world can't buy that.

Travel Partners

When traveling adventure-style, going solo is great. Two is great. A family is great. Any other combination, you'd better be sure about it before you go. What my Dad used to say about organizing family excursions also applies to travel: "The time it takes to do something is multiplied by the number of people involved."

While traveling, singles always meet other singles, unless they choose not to. It's the same with pairs of friends and married couples. We've met and traveled with both singles and other couples, and made some great lifelong friends. It's one of the biggest benefits of traveling. You can't help but want to travel and stay in touch with other independent people who've dared to pull off the same kind of adventure you have.

Unless you already are a close, stable group of friends before planning to hit the road together for an extended period of time, avoid doing so. The swirl of excitement and the magnet of exotic places can pull loosely knit bands of travelers into different directions, compromising everyone's time and possibly causing conflicts. Traveling is supposed to be fun, so be sure to have some basic agreements with your traveling partner(s) ahead of time.

No matter who you travel with, agree on three things: 1) that everyone needs some time alone, 2) that there are certain activities you each want to do or accomplish, 3) that you'll take turns, if you have different things you want to do but don't want to split up for the day. "I'll go with you to the art museum, if you come with me to the glassblowing village."

Handicapped Travel

Adventure traveling as a handicapped person is more challenging, but no less rewarding. Depending on your disability, you can raft rivers, parachute, ride elephants, photograph wild animals, scuba dive, and explore jungles like anyone else. If you live without assistance from another person, you can very likely do the same while traveling overseas. Conversely, if you require an aide or family member or friend at home, you'll likely have the same need on a trip. The presence of a disabled person with a wheelchair or other equipment is not usually a barrier to interaction with locals.

Naturally, handicapped persons may have special questions. For more information on handicapped travel, write: Accent on Living, P.O. Box 700, Bloomington, IL, 61702, (309) 378-2961. This organization has general information on disabled travel, plus a free directory of firms offering specialized tours and adventures.

Families and Children

Traveling with children takes extra planning but most parents who do it report great trips. Kids can adapt better than we give them credit for, and taking children to exotic locales and little-known destinations is now common practice. Often, children act as instant ice-breakers between travelers and locals.

General health and safety remain a constant concern for parents. First, there is the lack of certain anti-bodies built up by young children, which eliminates some countries from your itinerary. Children require constant monitoring, regular diversions, and continuous entertainment, which can impede a parent's relaxation. Then there's the nuisance and noise that tired, cranky, or energetic kids can create. But we've met families on the road everywhere, and invariably their kids have had a great time.

The lack of common spoken language between kids and others doesn't get in the way of the fun. I remember one little Scandinavian girl of about four at a seaside restaurant who drifted over and chatted with us for several minutes in her own language. Very gleefully she described something she'd seen—hands motioning this way and that—and we rolled with her, kind of nodding and repeating some of her words, as if to say "Uh huh, go on..." She finished and happily bobbed off back to her table, assuming we'd understood the whole thing. We hadn't comprehended a single word!

For more on traveling overseas with children, see the bibliography.

Making Big Plans To Go 4

The blue nutmeg pigeon of Banda, in the Molucca Islands, lives on nothing but the aromatic spice.

▲▼▲▼▲▼▲▼▲▼▲▼▲▼▲▼▲▼▲▼▲▼▲▼▲

A Southeast Asia man has focused his "ki" energy to the point that he can light paper just by holding his palm over it. This has been filmed.

▲▼▲▼▲▼▲▼▲▼▲▼▲▼▲▼▲▼▲▼▲▼▲▼▲

Bula® brand surfwear comes from the Fijian word mbula, or "hello." Billabong® brand surfwear means "swamp" in Aboriginal.

The planning stage is accelerating. Let's eavesdrop on a typical conversation inside the typical mind: "...Money, credit card, insurance—check. Physical, shots, teeth examined—check. Head examined—check. Yes, I'm crazy. Next, the cat, the dog, the house, the car, the folks, wait a second—my job, my name, my security! What am I doing?! (Relax. You've told all your friends. You have to go now.) *Alright, where was I? Traveler's checks, first aid kit, insect repellent. How long can I really go?* (Sell the stereo and you can go another two months.)"

Figuring Your Departure

Amount of Time

If you've decided to go, congratulations—you're bound to have an incredible time. The next step is to decide for how much time you should go. The easy answer is for as long as you can afford it. People have all sorts of reasons why they travel. But because you only live once you might as well go for as long as possible.

The shorter the trip, the sooner you'll be heading back home, and—if you work—heading right back to work. The less you'll have seen, the fewer incredible experiences you'll have had. You'll be paying good money to go somewhere. Getting there and back is by far the greatest single expense of any trip. So stretch out that expense over several months or longer. Enjoy the investment by staying for as long as possible.

Introductory exploring takes at least a month. Serious foreign exploring requires three months or longer. This of course depends on how much traveling you want to do. Some people just go and decide to come back when they feel like it. Others work en route to fund each leg of the journey as they go. My recommendation is an absolute minimum of one month per country visited. Many countries—like India or Mexico or China or the independent republics of what was the Soviet Union—are so diverse that you could easily spend years exploring each.

If a year, six months, or even three months sounds like too big of a commitment, experiment with four to six weeks in one distant, exotic place. That may give you the confidence to go for it in a bigger way later. But be warned: as friends and fellow travelers have confirmed, deciding to travel for only a few weeks may make you wish you'd stayed longer.

Reviewing Alternatives

Part of deciding to go on a foreign adventure is having the will to sacrifice. It's hard passing up other opportunities in order to travel. It's hard to leave your comfortable life, your relatives and friends, your pets, your security, opportunities at work, the chance to make more money, and the pleasure of your possessions. Disengaging from family expectations is hard, too.

If you're not waist-deep in a career, you're in the clear. But if you do work and feel like taking a break, it's never too late. You'll have to grant yourself permission. You'll have to save money. You may try to pin a value on it or assign a merit level to adventure travel, and discover it's about as easy as nailing jello to a wall.

But most people who have done independent adventure travel and enjoyed it agree: travel provides constant refreshment. It gives you the chance to drop old patterns or revive them. Indeed, some feel travel reinforces the value of life itself.

New responsibilities in your job, a new place to live, a new personal relationship, a new school, getting married, starting or having a family all offer their own advantages. I'm not about to convince a just-graduated propulsion engineer to turn down an offer from NASA. But I feel more fulfilled every time I travel, no matter where I was career-wise before I left. It may help to look at your life as a forest of chances, not just a single tree.

Set aside some time to think about it and you'll gain a powerful satisfaction having taken the reins and made your own decision. Then move on and settle your affairs. With everything tidy at home you can travel with an easy mind. That's the only way. Let's start with how you're going to bankroll this enterprise.

Arranging to Leave Work

Planning the Date

Unless you just won the lottery or have come into a big inheritance, you're probably funding this adventure yourself through savings from work or investments.

Let's assume your job is satisfactory. If you think you want to return to it, look into taking a paid leave of absence. If this is not possible, look into unpaid leave. Either way, write a proposal and present it to your

At these moments, the last things you want are lingering money or health worries. Settle them in advance. Carriacou, Grenada, West Indies.

boss. If this option is not available, try to leave with a written agreement that you'll get a chance to re-apply to your company if you return within a certain time period.

Even if you love your job, extended foreign travel may change your perception of it or of your career. So leaving it all behind and departing with a clean slate may help you get the most out of your overseas experience. Your category of work may be easy to get back into, or it may not. This distinction might be the core of the question of whether to go.

Give notice only when you're really ready to leave your job. While you may think it's preferable to give as much as two months or more notice it's not usually required. In some cases you might even get a negative reaction. Instead of being appreciated for giving, say, six weeks' notice, you may be asked to move on sooner so you can be replaced. Each situation is different, so be sure to remember your needs along with your employer's. Two week's notice is standard practice.

Returning to Work

When we last returned from a long trip it was relatively easy for us to slip back into our occupations. You may be leaving for a short enough period that you can return to your current employer. If not, it is true that more and more companies appreciate travel experiences. Simply listing it on your résumé can get you noticed, and it may interest an employer who appreciates an independent spirit. It also can be an interview icebreaker. For example, my wife Kerry once had to re-direct a job interview back to the subject when the interviewer continued to talk about Kerry's trip!

Making Ends Meet

Are you leaving work for good? Ideally, you've left some funds to live on for awhile once you return. A healthy savings will let you take the time to hunt for that just-right position. But if things are tight or if you don't want to touch your savings, relax. It's never been a problem for us to earn enough to live on. You can stuff envelopes, freelance or contract in your line of work, or pick up short-term assignments through temporary agencies. Temporary or seasonal jobs can expose you favorably to a potential employer, and add experience to your résumé.

You could trim some food costs while job hunting by part-timing at a restaurant where your shift may include a meal, or by stocking shelves at a store. Or how about a couple of evenings at a clothing store where you get discounts? Or offer to trade your repair or landscaping skills to your landlord for a rent reduction. Work is out there to keep you going until you get a full-time job in the area of your choice. If you've got many years of professional experience it can be even easier to find work again. Plus, you can consult independently, which may turn into a position or become a full-time business. Be flexible and don't be snooty about what work you'll accept, and the transition back to a satisfying full-time situation will come more easily.

Determining Available Funds

Financial Overview

Getting ready to leave means tying up loose financial ends ahead of time so there's as little as possible on the home front to occupy your mind. You want the maximum energy to apply to traveling, not worrying about what you left behind. It starts with counting your gold pieces.

You may or may not have a complex financial portfolio. Either way, stick to basics. Boil down all your money into four categories, called Now, Depart, Later, and Won't Touch. Condense your Now money (the money you'll be living on from now until you leave) and your Depart money (what you'll take for the initial part of your trip) into one checking account and one savings account.

Designate a family member, friend, or financial adviser to manage your Later money while you're gone. That is, the money you're keeping in reserve at home to draw on later. Place this third category of money (Later) into a short-term vehicle, such as a short-term, automatically renewing CD, money market fund, or low-risk mutual fund. These will pay interest or income but remain liquid so you can get at them from some exotic, far-flung locale.

As for your Won't Touch money—the long term investments you won't raid while you're traveling unless you suddenly decide to buy some splendiferous antique—let them stay put in various longer term CDs, stocks, and/or mutual funds. Assuming these monies are more aggressively invested and will be more drastically affected by the whims of the marketplace while you're away, diversify. Consult an investment advisor for advice, then arrange to have the funds re-invested upon maturity in your absence, or managed, if you decide not to manage them yourself. This depends on how long you'll be gone, of course, and whether you or someone else will be making your financial moves. If you're something of a gambler, and want to expose the speculative portion of your Won't Touch money to higher risk while you're gone, do it. But be prepared to not be able to react to market changes as quickly as you'd like.

Financial Control

If you plan to control your assets personally while you are away, you'll be making long distance calls, writing notes, or faxing details, and will need confirmation of your decisions. This will interrupt your travels if there's a hassle or a communications problem, and will jar you out of your travel dream. One way to get around this—other than designating someone—is to assign an international bank or brokerage firm to manage your funds. That way you can stop in and say "hi" and check on investments whenever you pass through a major city.

Power of Attorney

You'll need to have a power of attorney (POA) form drawn up that allows a friend or relative to make financial decisions in your absence. Specifically, this means the person keeping an eye on your Later and Won't Touch funds. This also allows them to pay your bills from your bank account. They also can pay your credit card bills and the bills that the traveler's check company sends for checks purchased while on the road.

Getting this POA form taken care of is easy. For the computer-literate, it's all available on software, or you can get the blank forms at a stationery store. Call an attorney if you know one to review it, or consult a

Legal Aid office. The form should be notarized. The power of attorney arrangement lets that person make decisions for you when you can't be reached, or if you're swinging in a hammock in Zanzibar and don't want to be reached.

It also ensures that no one else can touch your assets without your approval.

Access to Assets

If you don't know of anyone off hand to manage your funds, you can go to a brokerage firm and they'll arrange wiring funds to you when needed. At the least, a banker or brokerage firm person can advise you on what to do. You can get good advice simply by phoning the major firms, as well as getting information on international offices and telephone numbers. Try Charles Schwab, Fidelity, Prudential Bache, Merrill Lynch, or others. You should get some answers tailored to your portfolio size and investment strategy.

Generally, make it easy. If you'll be spending up to a year away, put your funds in fairly sleepy, stable places, and let someone keep an eye on them. You can call them regularly for status reports. If you have a lot of money, let an outfit look after it and tell them you want to get a certain percentage return while you're gone—like eight to ten percent—and let them perform.

Long-Term Leave

If you leave for longer than a year, your whole financial picture needs to be examined. You'll need to talk to a certified financial planner, a tax accountant, and an attorney, all of whom can advise you on investing and major estate planning.

Money Management Methods

Traveler's Checks

Paper money and coins you carry can't be replaced, so traveler's checks were invented. Traveler's checks are actually insured money. When you purchase checks you're typically (but not always—see below) charged one percent of the value of the checks. This fee is for the ability to have your lost or stolen checks fully replaced. One negative of traveler's checks, however, is that the money you pay for them does not collect interest.

Upon leaving, you'll need a few hundred dollars in traveler's checks, the safe alternative to carrying cash. But that's all, because you can get the rest while on your trip. Your bank or the check institution itself should sell them. The American Automobile Association (AAA) and other travel and financial institutions sell traveler's checks for no fee. Denominations should be in $20s and $50s, with a few $10s thrown in. You'll be given a carbon receipt that you should keep separately from the checks. This will help replace them if they are lost or stolen.

When you run out of checks on the road you can get more at any reputable financial institution. Whether purchased before or during your trip, American Express, Citicorp, VISA, and Thomas Cook are reputable companies, with worldwide offices. Keep a record of time, date, place, serial number, and denomination of checks cashed or spent. Send a copy of this record home every few weeks so you have a duplicate list in a safe place.

Some traveler's check firms also issue booklets that include tips on currency exchange, metric conversions, worldwide office locations, time zones, and other helpful facts. For VISA's free directory, write Travel Directory, c/o Corporate Relations, VISA USA, P.O. Box 8999, San Francisco, CA 94128. For a free copy of the American Express Travel Companion, stop by any American Express Travel Office, or call (800) 528-4800.

Credit and Other Cards: An Overview

Plastic non-currency competes with traveler's checks for convenience and value. The field of wallet-sized convenience cards resembles a crowded, never-ending horse race. One card gains a length and leads the pack because of a new feature. Then another charges ahead with a burst of new services. Remember, there are charge cards, credit cards, ATM (automated teller machine) cards, debit cards, and multi-feature "smart" cards, all of which are increasingly being used.

Observe your credit limit and keep a record of all transactions. Purchases on all cards are electronically processed and will appear on your account within a few days. List them and send your records home so the folks paying off your card billings can check for unauthorized purchases. Compare annual fees, interest rates, and other services before you become a card-holder.

VISA, MasterCard, and Private Credit Cards

VISA and MasterCard are two major companies that license a credit function, essentially making them banks. Any card that says VISA or

MasterCard on it is a credit card, whether it be from your bank, an agent of the licensor, or directly from the parent company.

Carry a VISA or MasterCard card with as high a credit limit as you can for those times you'll be between cash points. It's also the perfect back-up if you're suddenly cashless. Purchases accrue interest on the unpaid balance from the day after final day of your monthly billing cycle. You can carry a balance owed if you pay a minimum amount, which fluctuates with the amount charged to your card.

VISA and MasterCard let you get cash advances at most banks worldwide. You'll pay a cash advance transaction fee, and—unlike regular credit card purchases—you'll accrue interest from the day of the advance.

Credit cards, besides being convenient, have power because they are money. They are sometimes more trusted than cash or traveler's checks. Many travelers like the protection a credit card offers, like the option of disputing a billing if the service or merchandise you purchased does not satisfy. Often, credit card firms offer several kinds of insurance useful to travelers as part of the card fee. A credit card also can be flashed to border entry agents to show that you have the "sufficient funds" many nations require of entering travelers.

A Gold, Premier, or Silver version of these cards may provide added benefits like car insurance, improved purchase insurance, medical benefits, and so on. Also look into credit cards that have a mileage or other reward component. Some cards give you a mile of free air travel for every dollar charged.

Naturally, you need to maintain a checking account at home in order to pay off credit card balances. Try to set it up as an interest-earning checking account that you or the person you designate can write checks on to pay bills.

A way around this glitch is to send your credit card company a large amount of money before you leave, against which charges will be deducted. The drawback is that this money does not earn interest. You also now can use some credit cards as debit cards. This means you can use your credit card to withdraw cash from ATMs as you go,

> If you're temporarily low on funds, improvise. We cut it pretty tight at the end of one trip. Not wanting to purchase more traveler's checks, we bought our final day's meal before climbing on the plane home by emptying our packs of several paperbacks, for cash.

and enjoy the ATM exchange rate rather than the retail rate. (Retail means inside the bank or at a money exchange booth.) You'll still incur a cash advance service transaction fee but the money gets charged to your credit card account. All credit cards used at ATM machines or in a bank for cash advances accrue interest from the first day.

Private credit cards include gas cards (Texaco, Exxon), retailer cards (Bloomingdale's, Nordstrom), and business executive cards (Diner's Club, Carte Blanche). Unless you've already used these private cards in overseas adventure travel you most likely won't use them now.

ATM Cards and Debit Cards

If your checking or savings ATM card has the Plus, Cirrus, Star, or another ATM electronic funds network provider brand name on it, you can use it at any ATM worldwide with the same name on it. This lets you withdraw cash from your home bank accounts. Whether or not you pay a fee at home, you will pay a small, fixed transaction service fee no matter how much you withdraw. There may be an account fee structure and maximum daily amount available related to using your card. See your brochure for details.

If you plan to carry an ATM card memorize and write down the code in the standard phone pad set of letters and numbers—not exceeding four of either—so you can use any ATM. ATM buttons sometimes have just letters or numbers.

Bank debit cards, fairly new, basically are charge cards used against your bank accounts. They serve as a "plastic checkbook" in that they can be used to buy things instead of writing a check. The amount gets automatically debited from your home bank account. Debit cards also can be used at ATMs for instant cash, which also is deducted from your home account.

American Express

American Express is a diversified travel services company with a smorgasbord of services you may or may not use. Best known for actor Karl Malden leaning out of your TV saying "don't leave home without it," American Express is worth looking into.

The American Express Card in its Green, Gold, and Platinum forms is a charge card, not a credit card. This means the balance is due thirty days from when you purchase something. But AMEX now has a "Sign and Travel" feature for transportation tickets only that lets you bolt on a credit feature when you choose (after you've been a member for ten months).

Kicking back and relaxing on a big adventure may mean renting out or moving out, storing belongings, and an unpaid job leave.

S&T enhances the charge function, making this an optional, restricted-use credit card. AMEX also has a newer Optima card, their full-featured credit card.

To purchase traveler's checks from an American Express card while on the road you can go to an AMEX travel office. You'll have to supply your bank account number in order to get the checks. The cost is charged to your home checking or savings account, and the balance must be paid within thirty days. You also can use your card for cash advances from participating overseas ATMs, called AMEX Cash Express machines. You pay a cash advance service transaction fee for using these, and AMEX bills you on the next statement.

Along with traveler's checks and cards, AMEX has a cardmember mail-holding service, a travel agency/travel services function, a traveler's insurance feature, an emergency funds feature as part of a service called Global Assist, and more.

Smart Cards

Distant, off-beat cultures that adventurous travelers visit like to be paid the old fashioned way: in cold, hard cash. Sometimes they will accept travelers checks and credit cards. On occasion, they may barter.

But "smart" cards are heralding a new wave of money, complete with its own technology. Some people travel to get away from symbols of progress such as smart cards. Others enhance their sense of adventure and freedom by carrying one.

A standard smart card might be a credit card, with an ATM withdrawal capability, that also has a hologram on it to prevent counterfeiting. Upcoming cards will amaze even the most future-minded, and are limited only by the microprocessor inside. These include cards with all of the above features, plus an encodable, replenishable money amount that can be "spent" as the card is slid through a scanner. Expect to eventually see long-distance telephone time included, like with the phone cards already being used in Japan. Possibilities include any type of encoded information that lets a card act as a "key," so users can access money portfolio accounts from around the world, do transactions, pay bills, or even "card on" to a local computer interface to access e-mail messages and direct on-line costs to be debited from a home bank account.

United States Currency

It helps to have a few U.S. bills with you when you leave. For example, bring two or three $50s and a few $20s. Several $1s are good too, for taxi rides and tips when you're getting started. U.S. currency is very valued abroad in off-beat and Third World locations, despite its fluctuations. In many places people view it as safer than their own currency. You may be in a situation where buying something with U.S. cash gets you much more than a U.S. traveler's check or local currency would. Furthermore, in the unlikely event that you have to bribe yourself out of a compromising situation, having cash to spend helps. For example, a ferryman will take you but not your backpack from the island back to the mainland unless you pay him an extra something in U.S. greenbacks. We've never had it happen to us, but we've heard stories. It's best to be prepared.

And when you come home it's always nice to have U.S. cash on hand for the first day or two.

Foreign Currency

Foreign money is just like U.S. money in that you can't replace it if it's lost or stolen. So treat it like the cold cash it is. And be sure to save some of the fun-looking money for souvenirs. Some countries have elaborately designed bills with photos, patterns, and lots of colors, bigger in size than our bills, but worth about a nickel. Or there's the Cook Islands coin dollar, with the noble, coiffed, tiara-adorned head of Queen Elizabeth II on one side, and Tangeroa, the male Maori tribal god of fertility on the other, shown gloriously buck-naked.

Currency Exchange

Unless you read or are firmly advised otherwise, buy a bit of local currency at the airport or port that you arrive in, not before. Most have a twenty-four hour exchange window. This will cover your initial taxi or bus ride, local phone calls, some food and first night's lodgings. Then, when rested, head to one of the big bank branches or money exchanges for a larger currency purchase, being sure to shop around a bit for a good exchange rate.

Most of the time, a currency's exchange value plummets once you depart its home country. Exchange your cash before you exit a country, either at a bank or the airport. You may be able to exchange it right there for the currency of the next country you're heading to. Otherwise you'll get only a diabolically small amount for it, even in the U.S. Exceptions to this rule are major currencies like Japanese yen, Swiss francs, British pounds, German marks, or Australian dollars, which retain most of their value.

If you're carrying a lot of a major currency but the U.S. dollar has risen sharply since you bought it, you may want to hold onto the money until it rises in value against the dollar before exchanging it back again.

Calculators

Take a lightweight, small plastic calculator with you. In remote places they're still conversation pieces, particularly the solar powered ones. You'll become a master at exchange rates and at getting the most value out of the money you spend. Plus, it's always fun to take out the old number cruncher to see just how little you're spending.

Income Tax Planning

Filing Returns

There are always two dates on the tax calendar to remember: the first, when you filed your annual IRS return (typically last April 15) and the second, the next time you will file (typically next April 15). If you leave and come back between filings, you should be okay. Hypothetically, if you file a return on April 15, leave on April 16 and come home 363 days later, and earn no foreign pay, it should be easy. You made no income other than perhaps interest or some other non-wage income, there or here. You still have time to file under the deadline.

However, if you'll be out of the country for any time—two weeks, two months, two years, two decades—and April 15 will pass by, the best thing to do is call the IRS first. Ask before you leave what the filing requirements are. If you can prove you will be gone they may grant an extension past April 15 if necessary. Confirm all phone correspondence. Get the name and location of the IRS representative you talk to, write it down, and follow those calls up with a letter confirming the contents of the conversation. Save a copy of the letter(s) for your files. Misinformation from the IRS is not allowable as a defense against missed deadlines.

Living and Working Overseas

As of this edition, if you're living and working overseas (not just traveling) you automatically receive a two-month filing extension. If you file a Request For Extension (form 4868) by April 15, or write a letter, the IRS can grant you a four-month extension. You can get a further two-month extension—thus totaling six months—if you then file an Additional Extension (form 2688), or write a letter. If you are simply traveling you can't get this additional extension unless you're able to prove a hardship condition. Whatever your situation, if you're unable to sign your return, a CPA, a family member, or someone with the power of attorney may sign for you.

Foreign Income Taxation

As a U.S. citizen, any income you earn outside the U.S. may be subject to taxation. Certain tax treaty provisions we have with foreign countries affect this, and the IRS can provide details by country.

It can help you to work for up to a year or more. As of this writing, if you have relocated your home permanently to another country or at least for 330 days of any twelve-month period and are working, your tax home is considered outside the U.S. This may qualify you for the Foreign Earned Income Credit, which allows you to exclude up to $70,000 of earned income from U.S. tax. Interest or investment income is not shielded.

Estimated Tax

If you're self-employed in the U.S. and you've been filing estimated taxes on a recurring basis, it should not surprise the IRS if you stop. You know you've left the U.S., and they'll soon know too. Whether you left to work or travel or both, the April 15 filing of your taxable amount is your declaration as a citizen that you either owe tax or should receive a refund, and this "denominated declaration" will justify the stopped quarterlies.

Audits occur to both wage and salary earners as well as self-employed people, for all types of reasons. The IRS knows people are leaving from and returning to the U.S. every day. If you play by the rules, you won't have to worry much about coming home to an audit. You can avoid taxation but you can't evade it. And even one hundred percent honest mortals get audited.

Normally, you must always at least file a signed return as of midnight April 15, with a check for tax due unless you're entitled to a refund. Any amount due and not included in your filing is charged interest.

Being a scofflaw, like filing late without explanation or without asking permission, or not filing at all, should be studiously avoided. They don't shackle you anymore, but if you're a big-income individual, well, debtor prisons are in operation as we speak.

Student and Teacher Savings Cards

Regardless of your age, are you enrolled as a full-time student, or have you been recently? Are you a teacher? In either case some organizations issue savings cards, like the International Student Identity Card, that earn discounts from trains, lodgings, theaters, and musical events, plus special insurance, medical, legal, and financial benefits.

These cards are available from The Council on International Education and Exchange (CIEE), (212) 661-1450, Student Travel Association (STA), (800) 777-0112, and others. You also can inquire at the student services center at your school.

Personal Health

Physical Overview

Books and people abound with great information on the subject of maintaining good health overseas. Here's a quick overview.

Generally, your genetic and bacterial make-up, patterns of living and eating, and overall physical and social environment are markedly different in the U.S. than elsewhere. Not necessarily better, just different. It's the same for foreigners coming to our country.

If you take care, you'll minimize your risk of running into problems and ensure your continued well-being. The greatest risk you're taking, and your greatest source of satisfaction, resides in the decision to break your pattern and take a foreign adventure. You're over the biggest hurdle.

For kids, fun and energy come easier with healthy meals, rest, diversion, and playful exercise. Nile temple of Karnak, Luxor, Egypt.

If you can do that, all the preparation for leaving and the active taking of precautions while traveling is easy.

Begin with a full physical. Don't forget to schedule it before you leave your job, so insurance will pay for it (assuming your insurance covers physicals). The same goes for shots, medication, refills, and so on. If you've had a physical within the last six months, skip this step.

See your dentist in plenty of time to have any necessary work done. Now's the time to have those procedures done that you've been avoiding.

Visit your eye doctor, foot doctor, gynecologist—all the medical types you normally see. Before leaving you'll want to have the confidence of a clean bill of health, and, if you have a medical condition, the reassurance you still can travel.

Traveler's Shots

You'll need a series of vaccinations (shots), and possibly a series of pills (called a regimen or prophyllaxis) before you go. Shots are available through your personal doctor or your county public health office. Or, look for traveler's clinics connected to hospitals, or in connection with university medical centers. They usually charge a fee for assessment, plus the cost of the vaccinations and pills. You also can call the Centers for Disease Control and Prevention in Atlanta at (404) 639-2572. Their International Traveler's Hotline offers updated information and recommendations on what types or shots, pills (like malaria), and general medical supplies to take.

Vaccination Record

As you get your shots or prescriptions record them on what traditionally has been called the yellow International Certificate of Vaccination. Your doctor should have blank ones, or call your county public health department for the proper form. Have it stamped or signed by the physician in charge. Some shots are good for ten years; others have a short viability or duration and you'll have to get them (or a follow-up booster) en route, many months into your trip. Determine this in advance. Once you know where you're heading, find out what shots you need. Ask about their period of effectiveness.

You may be getting some vaccinations on the road, or your travels might take you in a new direction you choose while en route, calling for special shots. In either case, look for a similar health authority in the country where you're traveling, and be sure they use new, disposable needles. Insist that you see the syringe and needle packets unwrapped in front of you or bring your own.

We got cholera shots after beginning one trip because we knew we wouldn't be in a cholera zone until later. "Later" would have been after the three month period of effectiveness of the cholera vaccine, had we gotten it at home. We did get gamma globulin shots at home before our last trip, but because the effectiveness is short-term, got the recommended boosters while on the road.

Carry your shot certificate with the care you would give your passport, traveler's checks, and cash. Sometimes you'll need to show this proof of vaccination to enter a country.

First Aid Kit

Put together a basic first aid kit, making sure to keep it light and small. If it can all fit into a ziplock sandwich bag, great. You'll want an anti-bacterial first aid cream, a basic painkiller salve containing corti-sone, upset stomach and diarrhea remedies, cold/flu tablets, some different sized bandaids in their own bag, lip sunscreen with zinc oxide, tweezers, and a cream to combat basic skin rashes or fungus (non-prescription compounds containing tolnaftate or chlortrimazole are best).

Bring aspirin for pain, ibuprofen for swelling or cramps, and ideally some codeine for serious pain. Take penicillin and/or sulfa drugs if you are prone to tonsil or bladder infections. A prescription antibiotic as a back-up is important for fighting stubborn infections, but take it only when other methods fail. Consider a small snakebite kit. See the appendix for a complete list of first aid items.

Repellent and Sunscreen

Additionally, you'll want to carry insect repellent with high percent-ages of toluamide (popularly called Deet). Get sunscreen with a sun-protection factor (SPF) of at least fifteen, if going to the tropics or high elevations. Carry water-proof sunscreen or lotion if you'll be doing activities like snorkeling, surfing, and swimming. Sun-sensitive travelers may be interested in special protective clothing. One manufacturer of these products is Sun Precautions, 2815 Wetmore Avenue, Everett, WA 98021, (206) 441-6688.

Personal Medical Needs

If you have a personal medical condition requiring regular medication, take a supply of it for the whole trip. Carry a day's supply on your person, and the rest in your backpack or duffel bag. You should arrange with your doctor to have more sent by overnight air express if you need it. If so, make a call directly to your doctor before you leave, and make sure they know you might call from abroad. Arrange to have them send the prescription to a U.S. embassy or consulate en route, marked "Urgent/Medical."

Some legal prescription medications are illegal abroad, and vice versa, so ask your doctor or the embassies of the countries you'll be visiting about regulations. Carry a letter from your doctor stating your condition and giving permission to carry the drugs, and you should have no problem.

Leave your medicines in the containers they came in, with the original labels. Since drug names and compositions vary by country, also ask your doctor or pharmacist to write down the generic name, for when you need a refill. Never mix pills into one container, for the obvious reason of risk of misconsumption. Also, a border official may confiscate them.

As you might at home, carry a brief warning in your wallet or money belt if you are allergic to anything, or if you have a medical condition (epilepsy, diabetes, and the like) whose onset might preclude your ability to explain it. If your condition could be fatal without quick care, get the warning translated into the language of the countries you'll be in. A translation service, local college, embassy, or consulate can help you with this. Also, wear a medical alert bracelet engraved with your name, medical concern, and the full phone number of a person who can advise on your condition. One source is Medic Alert, P.O. Box 1009, Turlock, CA, 95381, (800) 432-5378.

Further, whether you have a special medical situation or not, you should carry a brief summary of your medical history. This might include past surgery, past or ongoing illnesses, and your blood type. If your history includes a recurring or present infectious or communicable disease, or if you are HIV-positive or have AIDS, inquire before leaving about any entry restrictions for the country you're visiting. Different countries have different rules.

Eyewear

Take a duplicate set of contact lenses or glasses, and the prescription, plus lens solution and cleaner. Better yet, take glasses alone so you eliminate the hassle of cleaning contact lenses. And make sure you have prescription sunglasses, plus a back-up pair of plastic snap-on, flip-down sunglasses that fit your regular glasses, just in case your prescription sunglasses break or disappear.

Locating Medical Help

Before you leave, you may wish to contact the International Association for Medical Assistance to Travelers. They supply names of English-speaking doctors in the areas of the countries you'll be visiting, immunization requirements, and more. The number is (716) 754-4883. Information is free, but they appreciate donations; the address is 417 Center Street, Lewiston, NY, 14902. You need to get a membership card in order to obtain an overseas referral .

If you get seriously hurt or ill while traveling, call or have someone else call the U.S. embassy or consulate. They'll help you locate the best medical help in your area. In some countries, medical care is free, and if not, they can see to it that money arrives from your family, friends or insurance carrier promptly to pay for medical costs. You also can call International SOS Assistance, P.O. Box 11568, Philadelphia, PA, 19116, (800) 523-8930. They offer twenty-four hour emergency assistance, referrals, and advice.

Any specific medical or health questions can be answered by your doctor, by medical books for travelers, and by the health section in travel guides for the specific areas you'll be visiting.

Insuring Personal Safety

Traveler's Medical Insurance

You'll need a medical insurance policy that goes anywhere in the world you do. Inquire of your current policy provider, or call around. Get an individual or couple policy or one that covers your kid(s), and be sure to pay the premiums in advance or as you go. If you are leaving an employer to travel, there should be a provision in your policy that extends your benefits for up to a certain time. This avoids the need to get re-qualified for a new policy. For example, one automatic extension called COBRA extends for eighteen months after you leave your job, allowing you to pay for what your employer previously covered. Be sure to read the fine print, as the U.S. health care industry is currently in transition.

Whether or not you continue on an existing policy or purchase or renew an independent one, be sure it covers airlifting, too. Outside European or other First World locations with Western-level healthcare systems you're often hundreds of miles from decent medical care. Be prepared. You never can be too careful with your health, particularly in remote locations.

Most health-maintenance organizations (HMOs) and Blue Cross/Blue Shield offer insurance that covers foreign travel. The American Association of Retired Persons (AARP) does also, and can be reached at (800) 523-5800. One independent provider is Travel Guard International, at (800) 826-1300.

Driver's Licenses and Auto Insurance

An International Driver's License allows you to drive anywhere on the globe. Some countries ask for it, others don't. You can get an application from any AAA office. Or, write: AAA, 8111 Gatehouse Road, Falls Church, VA, 22042, (800) 336-4357.

When you travel, also bring your driver's license from home. This looks official to those who rent cars or scooters. As for your auto insurance, it may not apply overseas. Ask your agent or AAA if there is a special additional policy for overseas driving that's required for your destinations, or at least available. This will help you avoid the surcharge that the scooter or car rental person sometimes asks for. Some credit cards provide auto insurance coverage as a benefit to using the card. Contact your credit card company for details.

Ask questions before you go. In far away places the law is often ragged, and drivers can be detained until accident damages are paid. If you're uncomfortable, have someone else drive, or take a bus or train, just to be sure there are no problems. Certain areas around the globe follow the rule of "s/he with the most money pays." This could well be you, even if you're not at fault.

Wills

If you're alert when you travel, there's usually no more chance of something happening to you than at home. Looking globally, it's clear that certain factors drive up the possibility of catching an illness or experiencing a crime. But in other places, certain factors drive the possibility down.

To provide for those at home you care for it's important to set up a will before you leave. While this may or may not be the first time you've thought about it, it's a sensible, necessary step to minimize what would be a trying time for friends or loved ones in the event something happened to you.

Generally, your money and possessions (your estate) will more easily and quickly go to those you designate in a readily accessible will or living trust. A will is simple to set up, while a living trust is a bit more involved. Will-making guides and forms are available in software or paper form.

Alternatively, you can approach your state legal aid offices, state or county Bar Association, university student legal services offices, or the attorney section of the yellow pages. Laws vary by state; you may or may not need an attorney to prepare a legally binding document.

Reducing Your Possessions

Personal Furnishings

Imagine you're a Galapagos Islands land tortoise. If you can't carry what you need for your trip on your back, on your bike, in a boat, or in a shoulder duffel, you'll have to sell it, store it, or leave it at your place. It depends on how long you'll be gone.

So if you have enough stuff for 300 land tortoises to carry, have a

> On longer trips plan to base yourself several days in an area, and do excursions from there, to conserve energy and budget. You can relax, explore, and minimize unpacking/repacking. You'll save money on transit, and enjoy cheaper multi-night lodging rates.

garage sale and get rid of everything you've been meaning to. It's a good cash-raising exercise. If you're a renter and going for a longer period of time, arrange to move out and store your belongings in a public storage place, or with friends you trust, or with relatives. Depending on your time away, sell your car(s), store, or loan them to friends or relatives.

Before our last big adventure, we had a massive garage sale. Then we stored most of our stuff—clothes, sports equipment, furniture, kitchen supplies, and stereo gear—at a storage locker. We sold one car via classified ads and loaned the second, gave plants and various other items to friends to look after, and made a couple of big donations to charitable outfits. It all went somewhere. And boy, do you feel free when you reduce your worldly possessions to the contents of a backpack.

Real Estate

If you own property, the decision is more difficult on how to manage them while you're away. Only you can determine whether to sell or not. Your situation is special, so make it work for you. Absolutely protect your long-term financial interests, but also remember you'll be far away. The more you leave hanging, the more you'll worry about while on the road. Renting out, selling, leasing, property management...all the possibilities should be looked at. Talk to a realtor and to a tax CPA. But do something, and then look forward to forgetting about it for awhile. If you've made good money on a place, sell it and travel on part of the profit. Then return and buy another place with the balance.

Remember, if anything major happens to any of your properties, your insurance policy is supposed to cover it. This may help you not to worry as much.

Short-Term Home Protection

You're in a gray area when it comes to briefer trips away from a home you own. Not a long enough time to rent out, unless by chance someone needs a home for a month or two. But still long enough to button it up properly.

If you're away for a short trip, ask or hire a trusted neighbor or friend to be watchguard, water the plants, feed the animals, bring in the mail, and if necessary, pay any bills. They may have the need for you to do the same in the future.

Renting

If you're already a landlord and you've arranged the tenant situation on your primary residence and any others, great. But should you own a place or places and need to rent them out, don't run an ad just yet. Start spreading the word among friends, through work, and to presumably responsible types, like medical or law students. There usually are bulletin boards at colleges and universities for precisely this reason. If you don't get results, put out a little cash and advertise. If a "just right" tenant doesn't come soon, try to offer reduced rent to a particularly responsible someone in exchange for looking after the place for you. Graduate student couples, families saving for a house, or older retired folks might be willing to do this.

Property Management Services

If you own one or more places you can have a property management outfit collect the rent from your tenants, ensure utility bills are paid, and find a new renter if one moves out. They charge a fee equal to a percentage of the monthly rent you're charging, in the ten to fifteen percent range.

House-sitting

Finally, there are house-sitting services, who screen candidates for you to select. The downside here is you usually can't charge a rent. If your home is paid for free and clear, a house-sitter is ideal.

Home exchanges

Doing a dwelling exchange with visitors from another country is another possibility, though exchanges tend to be for just a few weeks and can tie you to one area. Basically, you simply exchange homes and cars with someone who wants to visit your home town. One outfit out of San Francisco that reportedly is reliable is International Home Exchange Service/Intervac, P.O. Box 3975, San Francisco, CA, 94119.

Pets

Deciding what to do with animals is a delicate matter and there is no simple answer. If you can leave yours with trusted neighbors, friends, family or a caretaker the whole time, this is by far your best choice. Be sure their medical records, medical needs, and neutering decisions are taken care of.

As for professional boarding, it's a possibility, but it is a jail sentence and the outside limit should be three months. After that, it's cruelty, and you're keeping the animal hostage to your nostalgia. At this point, with no one to take care of your pets and no humane alternative, as hard as it may sound, you should give them away.

Planning a trip in the future also means foregoing adding pets to your family today. As cute and cuddly as that puppy looks now, remember, it'll be big and lonely when you're away later. Avoid a tough decision and don't get that new animal until you return home.

Before our last trip we considered either boarding our two cats near my parents or shipping them to stay with a brother, but finally we paid $50 per month plus medical and food costs to some friends to watch them. This turned out to be the most affordable and humane choice.

Getting Ready To Take Off 5

Abidjan, Ivory Coast, just above the Equator, has an ice skating rink.

▲▼▲▼▲▼▲▼▲▼▲▼▲▼▲▼▲▼▲▼▲▼▲

The former Soviet Union has eleven time zones. China keeps the whole country on Beijing time, though it spreads across five time zones.

▲▼▲▼▲▼▲▼▲▼▲▼▲▼▲▼▲▼▲▼▲▼▲

Polynesians never wore coconut shells as bikini tops. A promoter thought it up after one too many pineapple punches. "Bikini" is the name of a West Pacific atoll, though.

Passport, visas, ticket to ride, and a willingness to travel for a lot less than you live on—those are the basics. But of course, there's also that clothes issue, unless you're traveling strictly to the world's growing, clothing-optional resorts. And you'll need a good backpack. If you're headed to tropical beaches, you've got to be alert for getting wet. Better bring a mask, snorkel, and maybe fins. But what if your trip takes you to Tanzania's Mt. Kilimanjaro, too? It may sit at the equator, but you'll actually need snow gear.

Planning Your Travel Budget

Cost-Estimating

Can you economize, resist temptation, and live simply? Then as a solo traveler in off-beat or Third World locations you can live comfortably for $25 a day on a six month long trip. A couple can live for $40 a day. Of course these estimates exclude the cost of getting to your destination. And double those figures if you want to splurge frequently, buy a lot of gifts, or rent your own transportation often. Triple the costs if you want all the luxuries possible within the category of budget travel.

Go for fewer months, and the costs rise twenty-five percent per day, as short-term adventure travelers tend to fill their precious days with more activities. Go for longer, and the costs drop twenty-five percent per day, because costly activities tend to be spread out over time, and because longer-term travelers take days off from active exploring.

Your average daily cost per person includes three meals, lodging, and transportation fares. You'll also have to consider incidentals such as film, snacks, postage, entrance fees, event tickets, and so on.

To get started on figuring out your travel budget, add up your monthly home budget. As long as you're staying at inexpensive lodgings, eating at small street stalls and eateries, avoiding expensive restaurants, or buying food from public markets and cooking yourself, you can lodge, travel, and eat for *at least* two-thirds per month less than what you spend at home. And often much less than that.

On our last trip we spent about $300 each for a month in Thailand. We stayed in comfortable bungalow guest houses and ate out three times a day. The $600 we spent included transportation and $200 worth of silver

Traveling light with just a sturdy backpack, efficiently-packed, makes going anywhere a lot easier. Interlaken, Switzerland.

jewelry we bought. By comparison, traveling in Australia for one month we spent $700 each, simply by camping in a tent and cooking our own meals. Transportation was the big expense there, and rental cars were costly; it is indeed a big country.

Beyond the above savings there's a further difference when you compare cheap countries to even cheaper countries. Try to plan where you travel accordingly. And of course, remember the fail-safe method: have more money on hand or in reserve than you think you'll need, and you'll be fine.

Buying Power

Your travel books on individual countries will explain how far a dollar goes there. You can piece together a figure ahead of time with a little calculating. The Wall Street Journal lists the exchange rates of world currencies on a regular basis. Apply this knowledge to the expenses described in current destination guides, and you'll gain an accurate idea how much things cost abroad.

Your major transport cost to and from home is fixed, so the longer you're gone, the less your trip costs per day. But of course, the longer you're there, the more days' worth of expenses you'll have.

There are ways to cut corners. You can go by bike on part or all of this adventure, and avoid many transit fees. You can cook your own meals, bring a tent to camp in occasionally instead of paying for a bed, order appetizers instead of entrees, or eat only certain meals at restaurants. So split that soft drink with your travel partner, or buy food at the market and make your own lunch, or ride the open air truck to the hot springs or harvest festival instead of renting a scooter. It all adds up—or doesn't, if you economize.

Some people prefer to pay for extras—especially on a trip of less than three months—to maximize pleasure and entertainment. Others on longer trips are looking to really stretch dollars, and may be willing to rough it on a certain leg in order to splurge on the next one.

Always leave some extra money for special occasions. Birthdays, anniversaries, a special dinner or lodging after a week of particularly thrifty traveling, renting a taxi instead of lumbering slowly on a bus—it's good to reward yourself now and then.

Arranging Departure Transportation

Air Fares

Flying is the most common way to reach your destination, particularly if you have an ocean to cross. If you're a student or have been recently, are a teacher, or are under the age of thirty-five, try the Student Travel Association (STA) and the Council for International Education and Exchange (CIEE) for good fares. They've been in the business a long time so call them first. If you're not a student, you still might be able to buy from these organizations. There are plenty of other legitimate budget travel agents listed in the travel section of newspapers and in the yellow pages.

Discount Air Tickets

Bargain airfare hunting is an art and can consume more time than you'd like it to. But because round-trip transportation is the largest single expense of an affordable foreign adventure, do take some time to research your options before buying.

Don't assume that by calling an airline directly you'll find the most inexpensive ticket. Airlines are constantly—several times a day—setting fares, changing fares, and changing the price structures of individual flights. Calling an airline will give you a yardstick to try to meet or beat.

Unless there's a fare war or it's the off-season where you're headed, bargain fares tend to come from "bucket" shops or ticket discounters. These are low-overhead travel agencies that buy the unsold seats on various flights from travel consolidators. Consolidators buy various airlines' empty seat inventories in volume, consolidate them, then sell these seats to the discount shops, who in turn sell them to you at a discount.

Some discounters are reputable, others aren't. They are strictly selling the commodity of vacant chairs, and do not offer the extras that full-service travel agencies do. Nature abhors a vacuum, and so do bucket shops. They will lower their prices if there's an oversupply of seats, especially in the off-season. In larger cities, consolidators themselves will sell tickets, too, complicating the arena of just who to buy from.

Fare Ads

Look through the travel section of your Sunday newspaper and jot down the phone numbers of regularly advertised bargain travel shops. Or check the local yellow pages. Shop around, compare fares, and do your homework. Call the Better Business Bureau to see if a budget travel outfit seems reputable to them.

For shorter exploring (two to three months), buy a round-trip air ticket. For longer trips, only buy a one-way ticket. Often, the U.S. dollar is stronger overseas and will buy a less expensive return air ticket there than you could get stateside. We bought a return flight ticket home at the end of our last trip, and had no problem finding an affordable one that fit our schedule. However, it doesn't hurt to look into both round-trip and one-way airfares, as it's an ever-changing business with constant price battling. Some tickets are good for a year and you just have to make a return reservation when you want to come home.

One other consideration is the onward ticket. Some countries don't let you enter without proof of sufficient travel funds and an onward ticket. This either forces you to buy a round-trip ticket when you kick off your adventure or to purchase a one-way ticket to a destination beyond that country. Review your country travel guide for requirements.

Try to purchase tickets as close to the departure date as possible, yet far enough away to get the best advance purchase fares. Ask about and factor in whether the travel terms "high season," "shoulder season," or "low season" apply. Usually the "lower" the season, the cheaper the fare.

Absolutely use a credit card where possible. This will help you if you need to get a refund for any reason. Avoid any outfit that refuses your request to use a credit card. Ask for the total ticket price, which includes all taxes and surcharges. Ask if the seller is adding their own card surcharge, and if so, decide if it's still worth buying the ticket.

Always get the name of the airline you're flying from the seller before you pay, and ensure it's a confirmed reservation. Immediately call the airline directly if you have any suspicions; you should already be in their computer by the end of the transaction. Agree to be wait-listed only if it's free of charge; you should not pay until there is an available seat.

Transport Alternatives
Other Departure Methods

One method to save on international air costs is to hitch or buy a ticket on a cargo freight plane, freighter, or charter plane. But be sure to read ahead, and get ready for immediate changes beyond your control. These are truly adventurous methods, so if you have the time, go for it. But be sure to remember that you will be giving up certain conveniences for the privilege of saving money. For many, that's just part of the adventure.

Yachts and cruise ships occasionally look for crew members. Reading up on these situations or asking around a port will give you more information. You may be able to get paid for your on-board work, then get off at your choice of ports. There also are yacht delivery firms, and yachts going to or returning from a race, that you might be able to hitch a ride on.

The air courier business is a healthy and growing form of discount air travel. Air courier companies operate for shipping clients, and air regulations require courier firms to buy a seat on a commercial flight when shipping. They make money by filling as much of the available luggage space allotted to their purchased seat as possible. And who sits in the seat? The courier. You give up your luggage space (except the carry-on overhead compartment), and your ticket is paid for by the courier company. You sometimes can have as much as six months before you must return. Along with free flights, there are also flights where you split the ticket with the courier company or pay a heavily discounted fare.

Travel by Bike

If you like to bike, doing an off-beat adventure by bicycle can be superb. People are going for it all over the globe, both on road touring bikes and on mountain bikes. Either way, you're still able to use public transport because trains, buses, planes, taxis, and ferries will carry your bicycle. This lets you quickly cover large distances, then get off and bike around locally.

Biking enhances the adventurous component of your adventure. It lets you go where you want, when you want, and get right down to the people level. Foreign bikers cruising by are a curious sight, and it's a great way to increase local contact. Kids and adults alike will run alongside and want to talk to you.

When you go by bike you don't have to depend on local bus or train schedules, which frees your day up. You'll save money on lodging, because you can bike to secluded spots and camp. You'll stay in shape, get all the sun you want, and can explore just about anywhere. And if you want to stop biking, you can stow and lock your bicycle somewhere and come back weeks or months later. You also can sell it or ship it home.

Biking isn't all roses, though. Expect to get rained on, be chased by dogs, inhale bus fumes, get sideswiped by cars, and have breakdowns. If you bike it's also critically important to get rest and eat well.

In more developed countries the paved roads are better and a touring bike will work fine. Off-beat areas usually have bumpy and potholed roads, gravel roads, or dirt roads, so a mountain bike is a better choice. A mountain bike lightened of its panniers (saddlebags) also lets you trail-ride on day trips, too. Whichever form you use, plan on using front and rear bags and do not plan to carry anything on your back.

Talk to someone who's traveled by bike, catch a slideshow at an outfitter, and take some trial runs at home to be sure you like it. You don't have to be highly experienced, just motivated. Bring all your repair gear with you, and arrange for someone at home to be ready to ship replace-ment parts if you don't carry them with you, or can't find them locally. You or someone in your party must know the basics of bike repair.

Airlines will require you to collapse your bike and put it in a box. Pack socks or towels around the seat, gearing, forks, handles, and pedals to protect them.

Travel Documents

Passport

A passport is required to enter the majority of the countries on this planet, and for re-entering the U.S. A passport is valid for ten years from the date of issue, and registers you as a U.S. citizen with the government. While you're abroad, it's the government's job to know where you are so they can reach you or your family in case of emergencies, and generally to protect your interests as a traveling American.

A passport is the single most important document you carry as a traveler. Applying for one or re-applying for a new one is fairly easy.

First-timers must apply in person at a State Department Passport Agency, post office, or courthouse. Check your phone book under U.S. government agencies.

You Need to Supply:

- Proof of U.S. citizenship, such as a certified copy of a birth certificate or a certificate of naturalization or citizenship

- Two photos from your shoulders up, against a light background, 2" x 2" in size (look in the yellow pages under passport photos)

- Identification (usually a driver's license)

- Money. The fee is $55 for adults, and children up to eighteen receive a passport valid for five years for $40. Personal checks are accepted.

Renewing Passports

If you'd like to renew your passport, and it was issued after you were sixteen years old and within the last twelve years, you can apply by mail. If not, you're considered a first-timer. See above for how to apply. Write or call the nearest Passport Agency for the renewal form, or contact The U.S. Department of State's special mail-in center. Write: National Passport Center, P.O. Box 371971, Pittsburgh, PA, 15250. Fill in the form and send it back with your old passport. If you're reluctant to give up that hardy, well-traveled, dog-eared old passport with all those colorful visas stamped inside, don't worry, they'll return it to you with a "Canceled" stamp inside it along with the brand new one.

Allow yourself two months to apply for or renew your passport.

Additional Photos

If you are going to more than one country, carry ten to twelve extra passport photos of yourself. At many border crossings, as well as crossings between different regions or states within countries, the guards occasionally ask you to fill out a transit travel form, and include a photo, or you can't go on. As often as not, the nearest photo booth is days behind you at the last oasis, city, or jungle crossing, and border types *will* send you back. It may not be logical, as your passport photo obviously shows who you are, but look at it from their point of view. It's a little variety, it breaks up a long day of sending people onward, and it's a chance to exercise authority.

Realistically, they also need an entry record of who is where for safety's sake.

Transit Visas

Along with requiring a valid passport, many foreign countries require you to notify them that you'll be dropping in for a visit. They will grant you a visa that allows you to be there. This enables them to keep records of visitors, and to notify you in case of emergency. Make sure what's required; never depart home or arrive at any country en route without knowing the visa requirements! Often you'll be put on the next plane out—sometimes the same one you came in on—and that's no way to fly.

Frequently the country in question stamps the visa in your passport at the port of entry valid for one, two, three, or six months. Others require that you mail them (or bring along) your passport to their U.S. embassy or consulate prior to leaving home.

Types of Visas

Visa requirements change as often as political winds do. Up-to-date travel books for the areas you're visiting typically list visa requirements. A good travel agent specializing in budget and off-the-beaten-path travel should know the specifics of the countries you're planning to visit. You can call or write the embassy or consulate of the countries in question. Or you can ask Uncle Sam. Write for the booklet "Foreign Entry Requirements," Consumer Information Center, Pueblo, CO, 81009. Enclose fifty cents.

American nationals traveling abroad benefit from the world's least restrictive visa entrance requirements. The majority of foreign nations grant you a short-term visit—commonly a thirty-day tourist visa—upon entry. There are easy ways in many countries to extend it, once expired, to sixty days, ninety days, or longer. Non-traveler visa types include student visas, temporary worker visas, business visas, science/research/technical visas, and diplomatic/political visas.

But by no means do all nations make it easy to acquire or renew visas. Time or convenience may not always be on your side as you prepare to go on a trip. Fortunately, it is possible to get a visa—and sometimes more easily and for a smaller fee—in another country on your itinerary instead of in the U.S. It can take some doing, as you're a foreigner to both the country in which you seek the visa and to the granting country. But we've done fine in these instances.

For example, a friend once suggested that instead of the month-long wait in the U.S. to get an Australian visa we should get it in Fiji en route. It takes two to four days there. Our Canada-to-Australia air ticket allowed for a Fiji stop, so in the capitol of that island country we headed to the Australian Consulate and got the visa in a couple of days for free. We also once got Thai visas in a snap the day before entering the country from across the border in Malaysia. If you're in a hurry, keep these visa shortcuts in mind.

Also, some countries ask you to leave the country to renew your visa, then enter again. This takes time. Your travel guide should suggest efficient ways of doing this.

A friend's Dad was exiting Korea with two gift clocks. This struck the Korean guard as dangerously strange: "What's that?" "A clock." "Then what's that?" "Another clock." The Korean eyed Dad: "Why two clocks?!" "Well, one for wife and, uh—one for girlfriend!" Nods of approval, chuckles, suddenly no problem.

When obtaining or renewing visas, be polite, dress presentably, go early in the day, smile, and you should be fine. Asking around, talking with other travelers, or calling the embassy here or abroad usually will solve any remaining concerns.

If you are pressed for time, a visa expediter will collect your visas for you. Check the yellow pages first. By necessity, most are located in the greater Washington, DC area. Try Washington Visa and Travel Document Center, 2025 I Street, N.W., Washington, DC, 20006, or the Center for International Business and Travel, 2135 Wisconsin Avenue, Northwest, Suite 400, Washington, DC, 20007, (202) 745-3815.

Personal Travel Equipment

Choosing Luggage

I once ran into some forty-ish newlyweds in the middle of nowhere at a rest house off a dirt road on a sleepy tropical island in the South Pacific. They were so hell-bent on getting away and being romantic together in the lush undergrowth, off the crowded track, they forgot about backpacks. He was bent sideways, stumbling with an eighty-pound American Tourister hard-shell suitcase filled with hairdryers and electric razors and wingtips in ninety-five degree weather, and she had her arms slung through a metal Coleman cooler. It was packed with food they had brought all the way from Los Angeles.

They were great folks. They whipped out a box of Triscuits and a heavy aerosol can of Cheez-Whiz and we had a snack under the palms. Then off they went into the pages of history. Though blurred from the wedding frenzy and new to adventure travel, they still were having a blast. But I couldn't stop marveling at the hassle.

The key to comfortable travel is preparedness. *You must travel light.* This is the single most important tip in this book and is essential to maintaining energy and enthusiasm. You don't want to get fatigued, because it will affect everything you do. Each extra pound over your comfort zone can put you under an increasingly darker cloud, raining away your good mood. Along with minimized weight, your hands should always be free to reach a ferryboat railing as you leap on, or focus a camera, or grab your hat before it blows away.

Internal Versus External Frame Backpack

You'll need a light backpack, not a gorilla-proof suitcase. The decision comes down to internal versus external frame. The most durable is the internal-frame, tear-resistant cordura-style pack, with a supporting adjustable waistbelt. Some packs are two-in-one, where the pack folds, collapses, and emerges as a duffle bag. If you're going to be flying a lot this could be helpful. While an external frame pack provides better hip support for hiking, its frame is more prone to get caught on things. Unless you expect to backpack or hitchhike a lot on your trip, consider an internal frame pack. Most places in the world where you'll travel have buses, vans, trucks, boats, or planes. They'll carry your pack, not you. And when you arrive somewhere, the pack tends to stay at your lodging while you go off on local day trips.

If you don't know if you'll be hiking a lot, you probably won't be. But if you do plan to hitchhike a lot, or actually backpack across long distances, go with an external frame. Serious hikers know it's the more comfortable alternative.

Along with either frame style, you'll also need a daypack for carrying your valuables and other items during the day. Typically, you'll be based at an area for several days at a time, and not use your backpack or duffel bag at all. It then serves as the mothership, hovering next to your bed. Having a daypack—the shuttlecraft—lets you zip around on your local daily sightseeing without having to haul all your gear.

Some backpacks now have a removable compartment that's actually a takeaway daypack.

Locks

Locking your gear up, and locking it to solid objects, will keep it from being stolen. Look for packs that have zippers with holes so you can lock them shut. Purchase a few little brass locks for this purpose. Also buy a larger lock with a curl-up cable so you can secure your backpack to your bed or to a train station bench. Locks won't thwart a motivated thief, at home or away, but they do provide added deterrence against the casual pickpocket who's only mildly emboldened.

Neither of us have ever had gear stolen from our packs.

Clothing

Pick and pack clothes for the climates where you're traveling. You can read about weather in travel guides of the areas you're headed. Cotton or cotton blends are best for warm climates, and wool, down, and polypropylene are best for cold. No other artificial fibers will perform as well.

Naturally, in cool zones, you'll want to stay warm, and air conditioning isn't an issue. But in warm zones you won't find much relief in the adventure-style travel we're discussing. Generally, the only air-conditioning you'll know as a foreign explorer in hotter climates (except on a plane or in a modern building) will be Mother Nature's. That is, the cooling effect of a breeze as it evaporates your perspiration. Artificial fibers like rayon and polyester don't wisk away your moisture or allow the breeze to do its cooling as well as cotton.

Most travelers buy some neat new clothes as souvenirs on a trip. But if you need to replace torn or lost clothing, you should be able to find new or used men's and women's clothing just about everywhere, unless you're looking for high-end, expedition-quality styles.

Shoes and Socks

Nearly all adventure travel—except biking or kayaking—is conducted on foot, so you'll need quality footgear. Regardless of where you're headed, plan on bringing a good cross-trainer sports shoe, athletic sneakers, or a light hybrid. You can walk around towns and hike in the country with the same pair. Consider those with ankle support.

Bring a well-built pair of wet-'n'-dry river sandals, by Merrell, Nike, Teva, or Reebok. Quality flip-flops or thongs also will do, but barely, because of the lack of arch support. Don't bother with expensive dress shoes. Instead, men can bring a pair of light, slip-on loafers, and women can bring a light pair of flats or espadrilles. To save weight, avoid dress shoes, and buy a pair on the road if necessary.

Where it's cold, bring waterproofed and sturdy trail-hiking boots, already worn in. If mountaineering, a pair of rugged, supportive mountain boots is necessary, unless you're sure that you can rent boots for that portion of the trip. In all other cases, skip bringing boots. They're too heavy to carry.

Good socks are critical. Soft wool is best for all trips and all shoes, due to its comfort and breathability whether wet or dry, hot or cold. Quality cotton, tightly knit, is a close second choice. The theory to remember is that nature created us to survive with just bare feet in all environments except snow. You'll want the least amount of shoe and sock necessary to protect your feet from the elements, while leaving your gait unhindered.

Your most comfortable choice is to wear one pair of socks at a time, although wearing a thin silk or polypropylene liner inside helps some people. Too much sock, like wearing two or three pairs inside a shoe, causes heat build-up and friction, which can create blisters and swelling. Equipment stores sell special socks and shoe liners, as well as shoes designed for specific sports, and they can help with the details.

In my experience, I tend to wear sandals ninety percent of the time.

Special Gear

You may be heading to exotic locations requiring special gear. It's much cheaper and more convenient to take the gear along rather than rent it, as long as it's not too heavy. Follow your destination guides for tips on what you might be doing.

For example, if you'll mostly be in tropical locations, take along flippers, a mask with a plastic lens (not glass), and a snorkel. To save

Special gear, like a videocamera, may be worth taking. Viewing a replay, this Maasai in Kenya sees a picture of himself for the first time.

weight, split a flipper with your travel partner if you have one. We've split a pair and gotten along swimmingly.

If you plan to scuba dive and aren't certified, you can rent gear and get certified where you are. If you already dive and are certified, experienced travelers suggest bringing your own properly working regulator to ensure an accurate dive length. Tanks and suits are too heavy and bulky to carry.

If you're an artist, bring an extra couple of sketchpads, extra paint, brushes, colored pencils, and so on.

For areas where malaria is present, bring a mosquito net with a small spool of kite string and a few pushpins for stringing and hanging it up while you sleep. Malaria is transferred in the saliva of female mosquitoes as they bite, chiefly at night. Or, buy a net for less when you arrive in the country.

For dry or desert-like conditions, bring an extra bottle of moisturizer, extra sun protection lotion, an extra handkerchief, and a wide-brim cotton hat. For areas where you'll be experiencing a monsoon or foul weather, pack a light but sturdy collapsible umbrella and a light plastic poncho big enough to fit over you and your pack.

Special Transport

If you're on a trip with a particular emphasis, such as sailboarding the beaches of West Africa or mountain biking through Argentina, you'll have special travel and transport requirements. But the packing routine is the same. Bring it all and any required back-up supplies with you, unless you know through research that quality gear is available there. Call your airline or other transportation carrier to check baggage requirements. Arrange in advance for someone at home to send replacement gear by air, should you need it, or to forward gear to points along the way.

Two organizations can advise you if you're planning a long or elaborate expedition. Write: Explorer's Club, 46 East 70th Street, New York, NY, 10021, (212) 628-8383, or Expedition Advisory Center, 1 Kensington Gore, London, SW7 2AR England, (011) 4471/581-2057.

Rental Gear

If you have special gear requirements you may not have to buy any before you leave. Some areas rent travelers whatever they need. In Nepal, for example, outfits rent sleeping bags, tents, boots, and cooking equipment for travelers trekking into the mountains. Most tropical resorts rent sailboards, eliminating the need to ship your own. If you golf, don't bother lugging your clubs unless this is an adventure golfing tour (isn't that an oxymoron?) and you really must have them. There also are more and more local touring bike and mountain bike outfits in far-off places. Check your travel guide for details.

Gear Insurance

Along with cameras and backpacks, other gear could be lost or stolen, too. Check you homeowner's policy to make sure you're covered. Some policies allow ten percent of the total replacement value of your covered possessions to be lost or stolen away from home. This could cover anything taken overseas, avoiding the need to purchase an insurance "rider" for your trip. Some renter policies have a similar provision. Either way, take the time to read the fine print, or ask your agent. You may be able to purchase a temporary supplement just for the length of your trip.

You also can inquire about overseas personal property coverage policies from your credit card company, your travel agent, or AAA.

Money Belt

Say good-bye to your jewelry, wallet, purse, all those keys on a ring, and perhaps that pocket pen protector. Instead, buy a security money belt that snaps around your waist and rests against your abdomen. Use it for

> **If the water's bad, drink mineral water. But what if there's no water at all? A friend's parents were traveling in the former Soviet Union, and found no bottled water anywhere. So they brushed their teeth for three weeks with vodka.**

carrying your essentials: credit cards, traveler's checks, cash, passport, a little calculator, and other essential papers. You can get the flat kind and wear it under your shirt, blouse or jacket, or the belly pouch kind that carries more, such as film, glasses, or any medication you might need. There are other styles, too, such as arm, leg, and chest pouches.

Last Steps Before Departing 6

Wear sneakers in shallow water with coral. If it scrapes you, it continues to grow inside your cut.

▲▼▲▼▲▼▲▼▲▼▲▼▲▼▲▼▲▼▲▼▲▼▲▼▲

"Posh" comes from "<u>p</u>ort <u>o</u>ut, <u>s</u>tarboard <u>h</u>ome." During the Victorian era, first class passengers boating to the Mediterranean had rooms, coastline to gaze at, and cool shade all on the port (left) side. Going home, it was starboard.

▲▼▲▼▲▼▲▼▲▼▲▼▲▼▲▼▲▼▲▼▲▼▲▼▲

Kids on Baja's Sea of Cortez beaches find dead pelicans, spread their wings, dry them in the sun, then fly the light, desiccated frames as kites.

You've made your plans, your budget's arranged, and you're saying your good-byes. Your travel guidebooks are at the ready. In this chapter we review how to double-check news at your first destination, how to register something with U.S. Customs, and more. Are you absolutely sure the printed date on your departure ticket is the actual day you leave? Be certain. This is one wild ride you deserve not to miss. Are you feeling those butterflies yet?

Finalizing Your Departure

Travel Advisories

The U.S. State Department's Citizen Emergency Center hotline gives updates on political, social, health, military, and weather-related conditions around the world that may adversely affect your travels. The number is (202) 647-5225. Contact Citizens Consular Services at (202) 736-7000 with other questions, such as marriage rules for nationals overseas, adoptions, and legal assistance.

You can listen to the Center's advisories, get a mailed printout of the advisory, receive the information via electronic mail, or talk with a U.S. Consular Service person about a country. Advisories may be months or up to a year old, so don't be concerned with dates. These reports are updated as the local situation warrants, not necessarily on a regular basis. Double-check by keeping your eye on the newspapers. If it's an old advisory and you haven't picked up anything in the news, there's probably nothing of consequence to be worried about.

The State Department also issues health precautions and other information. To receive consular information sheets or travel warnings, send a self-addressed, stamped envelope with the countries or subjects you're interested in to: U.S. Department of State, Room 4800, Washington, DC, 20520.

Reviewing News

Grazing the international news in the months before you leave will let you travel confidently. While no one advises traveling into a war zone or other dangerous areas, remember that parts of countries may be quite serene while other areas of the same country are in turmoil.

Roads are sometimes bouncy and trying. Bring books, listen to tapes, or watch the scenery. Befriend a driver with snacks. Guangzhou, China.

Don't immediately write off a country you hear negative things about. Investigate further. Tourism may be down, but it could be because travel agents aren't currently recommending that particular destination. You're different—more intrepid, more adventurous. You may find that the trouble is localized, that it's a great time to visit the country because tourism is down, making it easier to roam without bumping into crowds, and to get more for your dollar.

Passing Through Customs

Inspection

U.S. Customs are the government folks who inspect, restrict, and impose fees or taxes on items you bring home. Having a smooth trip includes having a smooth encounter with Customs officials both when you leave and when you re-enter the country.

If you plan to buy a number of items on your trip, you may face some restrictions other travelers won't encounter. You can prepare yourself for the bureaucratic process by asking for the free thirty-page booklet called "Know Before You Go," which details current Customs regulations. Write: U.S. Customs, P.O. Box 7407, Washington, DC, 20044. Or call (202) 927-6724, their recorded information line.

Along with screening out goods, plants, animals, and agricultural products that are either illegal or carry damaging diseases, Customs officials levy a "duty" or tax on certain legal items you carry home. Basically, everything you bring back has re-sale potential, and Uncle Sam needs to know what is being imported in order to protect domestic competitiveness. Items from some countries are duty-free; others aren't. You're granted a certain duty-free quantity of personal purchases—called an exemption—on liquor or tobacco, plus a dollar amount that your purchases mustn't exceed.

When traveling between countries on your trip, it's a whole different ballgame. Some countries don't carefully monitor how much you bring in or take away. Ask other travelers on the road, or ask upon arrival what you can take when you depart. Make purchases at duty-free shops at departure ports and you'll find some good bargains on perfume, liquor, cigarettes, electronics, and more.

When you first leave on your adventure, register valuables like cameras, Walkmans, and videocameras at the airport or port's U.S. Customs facility. They'll give you a registration certificate, proving these items were with you upon departure. Having done this, you will avoid having to pay duty when you return.

Customs can get prickly. A friend's Mom packed some cactus, with spines, for her home garden. Plants are restricted, and it was touch and go when the U.S. Border Agent decided to open the suitcase and roam around with her hands. Mom lucked out.

Keep all your certificates and sales receipts for purchases made on the trip in one packet. You may be asked to show them later.

When you return, you'll need to prepare for Customs also. Just before you get on the plane, ship, or bus home, check your gear thoroughly for planted drugs or other illegal contraband. You could be an unwitting "mule" carrying hidden items, who then gets busted by Customs officials. Don't let this happen. Once you're at the port of entry, pleas of innocence won't get you far.

Customs Preparation

When passing through Customs it's normal to be nervous. Dental visits, traffic cop stops, and Customs visits all seem to present the same kind of anxiety. That's fine, as Custom officials know the difference between a person who is innocently anxious and someone who's hiding something. If you have nothing to hide, you'll be fairly calm and they will sense that. They'll also appreciate your honesty when asking you questions. This makes for a quick inspection, if they inspect at all. They'll ask where you went, for how long, what you bought, and so on. If they ask to inspect your luggage, comply.

If you do have duty to pay, either because you've exceeded your exempted amounts or you're carrying special or expensive items, it's usually a reasonable amount. Hiding an expensive purchase can lead to big consequences, where the fine and possible legal problems far outweigh the inconvenience of simply paying duty on an honest declaration.

If you've decided to become an importer on the trip, bringing back clothing, jewelry, antiques, or art to sell, you'll either be carrying it with you in person or shipping it separately. In this case, getting the Customs duty lowdown before you go is especially important. You will find out how much you can bring back while avoiding spendy tax surprises. This includes finding out the method for declaring goods you ship or carry home and which export-to-U.S. forms to obtain from the country where you've purchased the goods.

Besides airports, U.S. Customs officers also inspect at docks, cargo terminals, and at postal and air cargo entrance points. Trying to sneak in a precious item that you shipped home from far away—even in an innocuous brown package—will usually fail. It probably will be held at a Customs facility for you to claim if you pay duty.

Assuring Travel Security

Safety Attitude

When you're traveling in or out of a country you'll be spending a fair amount of time in airports, stations, and piers, waiting for flights, transiting customs, exchanging money, transferring bags, and so on.

It is highly unlikely your time in an embarkation site will be anything but straight-forward. Worldwide, airports are airports, train stations are stations. You are simply just one of the herd. But here are a few basic safety rules:

For ensuring calm, safe destinations, scan recent guidebooks and on-line travel chatgroups. Once arrived, ask of locals. Kavac, Venezuela.

Never leave your bags unattended or unlocked. Conversely, keep your distance from unattended bags.

Be inconspicuous while you're waiting to depart. Don't cause a stir—like cracking hijack jokes—or give any reason to be detained.

Don't agree to carry anything on to the plane, train, or boat for a stranger. And never carry weapons, volatile substances, or illegal goods—either yours or someone else's.

If you talk with the locals while waiting, avoid sensitive subjects like political affairs.

Notice where the airport or station's terminal emergency exits are, for general safety. In the very unlikely event of a terrorist attack while you're there, hit the ground. Head away from the scene if it's safe.

Remain cool in all confrontations. Don't make abrupt, jerky motions or "harrumphing" sounds as a sign of your impatience. Be passive, friendly, and agree to all requests. Gear and valuables can be replaced, but your life and freedom can't.

Overall, be patient while in transit. Transportation personnel are trying to process you and others safely and comfortably.

Time Zone Changes

Jet Lag

Boats, trains, and bicycles usually are slow enough to give you time to adjust to a new time zone. But when you travel at 600 miles per hour, jet lag kicks in. Jet lag means the plane seems to arrive a lot sooner than you, and you're lagging behind.

When you land, you're still on the same eating, sleeping, and waking patterns as when you left. You can minimize the toll on your body's natural time clock by getting into a new "normal" pattern as quickly as possible.

Try not to sleep much on flights because it may take you longer to adjust once you arrive. Stay away from big meals, eat lightly, and avoid anything with caffeine. Drink lots of water. If you're going to sleep on a long flight or a series of flights in an attempt to try to keep the wake/sleep/wake cycle going—or if you just fall asleep despite trying not too—don't drink alcohol. It keeps you from the deeper, most restful zones of sleep, holding you back from true revitalization. It will be hard to resist alcohol beverages, as they're often complimentary on international flights, but if you must, stick to beer or wine. Stash those free bottles of the hard stuff in your pockets, and save 'em to hoist in celebration of your arrival.

Stretch out a bit and walk the aisles to get a little exercise, too.

Body Readjustment

Once you're at your destination, switch to local time even if you don't feel like it. Go out for a few minutes in the morning light. At night, lay down and close your eyes in the darkness. This helps your body re-set its day–night biorhythms. You'll be excited to be in an exotic place, and you will feel "up" and consciously or unconsciously anxious about the newness of the whole scene. But try to allow yourself to sleep, and give yourself a few days to get the rhythms back. You can't force awakeness for long without the biological requirement of replenishing sleep, anyway; sleep for the body is as elemental as oxygen for the lungs. Go easy, restore your natural energy, and don't overdo it. Passing out in the middle of ordering dinner would not be a good introduction to the local culture.

Living On The Road 7

Woe to the shipwrecked sailor in Fiji in the 18th & 19th centuries. To stay, you had to throw a chief's javelin farther than him. If you lost, he ate you.

▲▼▲▼▲▼▲▼▲▼▲▼▲▼▲▼▲▼▲▼▲▼▲▼▲

Move your hand over glow worms in New Zealand caves, and they'll sense the heat and bend to it.

▲▼▲▼▲▼▲▼▲▼▲▼▲▼▲▼▲▼▲▼▲▼▲▼▲

New Guinea's Dani tribesmen wear a gourd resembling a long carrot over their private parts. And that's about it.

Amazement. This is where you pinch yourself daily because you can't believe what an incredible adventure you're having. Below are tips on making sure you have the very best time ever, whether it's your first off-beat adventure trip or your sixth. Covered are arriving, developing safe habits, avoiding crime, traveling at a comfortable pace, locating lodging, picking the best things to eat, and getting around. You're on your own, and look at you now: Indiana Jones or Amelia Earhart, move over.

Maximizing the Experience

Arrival Awareness

Arrival at a foreign destination can be both incredibly exciting and a tad scary. The wheels touch down, the boat toots and docks, or the train whistles as it enters the train station.

You hear strange words as you disembark and you notice the different kinds of faces and styles of dress. You manage to follow the directional signs and go through the motions of getting your gear and then, whoa. It hits you. You're actually here. Your many months of planning and imagining dissolve into the reality of arriving. It's exhilarating.

You begin to notice the environment: the buildings, the street scenes, the people, the color of the sky, the land, the trees. New sounds enter your ears. New music. New scents. New sights. You're on high alert, eyes and ears and senses dialed up full, receiving maximum input.

First Steps

You've got a lot to think about, so it's nice when your inner gyroscope takes over and you're on your way. You will find an affordable way to get to your first day's affordable place to sleep. Try to have a destination in mind by the time you arrive so you can drop off your gear in your room and get your bearings.

Once in a new country you'll want to cash some traveler's checks into local currency, and maybe find a copy of a newspaper in English, or a flyer that lists local happenings. Keep your eyes open for notices of festivals, arts events, excursions, information from other travelers, and so on.

If you've had enough time to memorize a few words or numbers in the local language, try them out. While the locals you're talking to may respond in English, they'll smile at your attempts to speak with them in their tongue. Who knows? They may well know what you mean on your first attempt and reply in kind.

Travel Pacing

A lot of travelers plan a long trip fully in advance. I did my first time. I arrived with an attitude. I had to be in the first country on the 3rd of the month, quickly to some town on the 9th, elsewhere by the 20th, then on to the second country by the 28th, because I had to be in the third country by the 12th of the next month.

I carried the notion of having to "get it seen" by a certain time, or my adventure wouldn't be a success. Until I learned the art of open planning, I was hustling from destination to destination like the cartoon Roadrunner, unable to savor truly remarkable places as much as I would have liked. Travel is about the heart, not the head. So don't fill your plate too full.

Day Planning

The whole point of an extended foreign adventure is to explore, and to let your plans fine-tune themselves at a speed that feels comfortable. Things like clocks and calendars and the working life make us good at applying artificially boxed-in time chunks to various labors. Your trip isn't a labor. It's supposed to be the opposite of everything from which you're taking a break. Leave the tendency to rush at home. It isn't necessary and will restrict your enjoyment of the pleasures and sights at hand.

Once you've arrived in a country, linger in the locations you like. Establish a base and take day trips from there. When you've covered an area to your satisfaction, move on to the next place and establish another base. Conversely, if a place seems empty or uncomfortable within a day or two, get right back on that train.

When traveling between countries, or on long connections to a new region within a country, keep it to that. Transit days are physically draining and will test even the calmest person's patience. Don't try to squeeze in exploration with these segments. Expect to have long transit days with border crossings, delays, and crowded train, bus, or boat transfers. Then, once you're in a new area, you can relax again and meander to your heart's content.

Avoiding the Obligatory

As travel is ultimately supposed to be fun, you're under no requirement to do or see anything you don't want to. The only requirement is to
get out of your adventure just what you want, including doing lots of
nothing. This is your trip, not the guidebook writer's, your children's, or
your parents'. Would you rather read the novel you just bought than see
that 500-year-old monastery with the 360-degree view? Do it.

Acquiring Local Information

Travel Advice

Keep your ears open for people who are coming from the direction
you're headed. They can sprinkle great gems of details—sometimes
accurate, sometimes not—that will supplement what you've read in your
guidebook. But don't plan too tightly—some of the best travel experiences
are embarked on spontaneously.

A certain traveler raves about a beach she's just been to, in the
opposite direction you're heading. Or there's a festival or village with a
great restaurant with entrees for sixty cents, or a mountain-top temple
draped in vines and mist, with monkeys hopping all over it, not covered
in any guidebook. Being able to flex to include unscheduled stops or
changes in plans will greatly enhance the fun you'll have on your trip.

Another good source of ideas for places to see nearby are postcard
kiosks. When you hit a new area, talk to fellow travelers who can offer a
fresh viewpoint, then look at postcards and read travel books to confirm.

Legal Awareness

When you step down the gangplank onto the piers in Singapore, a
sign reads, "Possession Of Fireworks Punishable By Caning." In Malaysia,
there's one that says "Death By Hanging For Drug Smugglers." Thieves
lose their hands in Saudi Arabia.

As in the U.S., if you follow the local laws you should be okay.
Fortunately, being a Westerner can be a benefit elsewhere, because many
countries count on our tourist dollars and don't want bad press. But it
pays to be cautious.

Bribery Awareness

If you haven't done anything illegal and you are stopped or detained,
don't panic. I once started panicking when a Mexican federale asked me

to follow him to the jailhouse after I made a U-turn. There was no sign prohibiting U-turns; the officer just wanted some extra money. So I started to reach for my wallet, but Kerry counseled me to wait. The officer held his hand through the window and said $20. I looked at Kerry, muttering about just paying it and getting out of there. Then the officer said, okay, $10. Then, "Cinqo, cinqo!" (Five dollars.) I pulled out a $5 bill and gave it to him and he drove away.

Bribing your way out of a situation has worked for people in a variety of situations. If you are particularly concerned, try to get the lowdown on this practice in advance from travel books or fellow travelers. Paying a bribe encourages harassment of future travelers, though, so avoid it unless absolutely necessary. I felt it was necessary as I didn't speak much Spanish and my visions of a night in a Mexican jail were not pretty, but with more experience I may have thought of an alternative.

Legal Counsel

If you do get into trouble, the nearest U.S. Embassy or consulate should be able to advise you. That's partly why they are there, to assist U.S. nationals overseas. They can help you find a lawyer, but they can't pay the fees for you. Otherwise, you basically are left to your own devices—especially away from big cities. The best advice is to stay calm and avoid situations your gut tells you aren't right. The vast majority of people you encounter overseas will be interested in you out of simple curiosity. But wherever you go, you're a long ways from the U.S. Developing that intuitive extra sense on the road can mean the difference between a great adventure and misfortune.

Crime

Criminal Activity

In every nook and cranny of the globe, there are bustling shopper's markets. In just as many nooks and crannies there are black markets bustling with hot credit cards, traveler's checks, passports, I.D. cards, cash, clothing, Western liquor, cigarettes, other consumer goods, and drugs. If you are going to play in that arena, you're on your own. If you're selling something, like a watch, a camera, a fancy pair of shoes, be sure you can before you do. You may be entrapped or found out later. Further, you may be deliberately befriended in order to get you to lower your guard, then planted with drugs or other illegal goods. Don't encourage these dangers by loitering in questionable areas.

Keep a low profile and studiously avoid criminal circumstances. If it's illegal at home, it's probably illegal abroad. Prisons can be primitive, officials usually will not speak English, the food and living conditions will be very unpleasant, the treatment could be inhumane, and the sentences for serious crimes typically will be stiff. As for drugs, see the film *Midnight Express* to get an idea of the harsh consequences of drug trafficking.

Restricted Sites

Observe signs and laws against photographing public sites, shrines, or security areas—specifically pictures of police, airports, military barracks, and industrial structures.

Theft and Security

Ensuring Safety

You may or may not have developed an advanced sensitivity to crime. It depends on where you're from and what's happened to you in the past. Further, the circumstances leading to the lack of or abundance of crime in one country are not necessarily different from those same possibilities in another. Los Angeles has creeps just like Buenos Aires or Bombay or Karachi. Conversely, almost every region on the planet has plenty of tremendously warm, welcoming locals.

The idea that harm is more likely to occur when traveling abroad than right in your neighborhood is both founded and unfounded. While the term "the boogie man" came from European sailors' encounters with Bugis pirates in the former Dutch East Indies over two centuries ago, things are different now. These days, you can let your fears go for the most part. Much is known and not much mystery remains about the folks you'll be mingling with and their particular behavior patterns.

Crime Awareness

Once on the road, though, you will hear and read about specific places that have reputations for thievery. It's important to be careful in these cases. While departing one country for another once, I left a camera and lens in a motel room, in a city known for lots of theft. We left at 4AM for an early flight, leaving our keys in the room and locking the door behind us, as we'd paid the night before. I climbed into a motorcab, went a few blocks, and realized to my horror what had happened. I dashed back and even at that hour our room already had been scoured. Someone had seen us go. No camera in sight.

This story illustrates that anywhere on the globe you will be watched even if you don't feel you're drawing attention to yourself. You are a foreigner and often will be presumed to be a good target. And I hate to say it, but the culprit could be a fellow traveler as well as a local. But with a healthy awareness you needn't be inordinately worried about theft.

Crime Remedies

If something like a camera or clothing has been taken, you can buy a replacement. If it's a passport, head to the nearest U.S. embassy or consulate to apply for a new or temporary one. If you're separated from traveler's checks or credit cards, follow the directions that came with them. They will tell you how to notify the issuing company, and you should have no trouble replacing whatever was stolen or lost. If you lose personal possessions, a review of your insurance policy will tell you whether they are covered. Review the policy before you leave home for better peace of mind. If it's cash, tell yourself that it's only paper with some colorful ink on it, and chalk it up to experience. Unfortunately that's your only consolation.

Back-up Documents

Be sure to copy all travel documents before you leave home, including your passport cover page with photo and visas, traveler's checks, credit cards, and all other important papers. If anything disappears, someone from home can fax you a copy. Make a second complete copy for each person traveling and carry those papers in a watertight ziplock bag tucked in the deep recesses of each backpack.

Overall Precautions

Here are some general precautions to take no matter where you find yourself or how safe everything appears:

- Let others know where you're going and when you're coming back.

- If you head somewhere with other travelers, agree where you're going and where to meet if you split up. Have a fallback plan in case you get inadvertantly separated.

- Did you meet a friendly person near your lodging? Don't give out your room number. Join them in a neutral place like a restaurant.

- If a taxi driver looks or acts suspiciously, don't get in. Be sure to agree on the fare before you accept a ride.

- After dark, travel in the company of others.

Carry cash, passport, and other papers in your waist pouch, neck pouch, shoulder pouch, or leg pouch, at all times tucked inside your clothing. As for expensive rings, earrings, and necklaces, leave them at home. If you must have these or buy them en route, store them in a safe at the front desk of a reputable hotel, or another place you feel is secure.

Just like in the good old U.S., pickpockets exist everywhere there are tourists. Be particularly alert in tight quarters like train or bus stations and on buses or trams. Some standard pickpocket tricks include slicing your daypack from behind and reaching in a chamber, being bumped into and robbed, or having your camera yanked off by a passing motorcyclist or bicyclist.

Any time you are directed to notice a stain or bird-dropping or mustard on your clothing, it's likely a scam to get you to remove your jacket or daypack, allowing a pocket to be picked in the confusion. Don't remove anything and keep walking. Fix it when you're sure the coast is clear.

Take off business stickers with logos or corporate names from your gear as long as it won't hurt your luggage. Use plain I.D. tags without company logos or business cards on them, as it's possible that company may have a bad reputation in the area you're visiting.

Thieves and con artists are very clever. You will be approached by people with stories of woe, funny stories, charming stories, flattering patter, "make big money," or "artifacts for cheap" schemes. Politely decline it all and don't stop walking. Also be careful of too-quick offers of chocolate, sweets, food, or invitations to places that sound suspicious. Knockout drops or powder can be used to incapacitate you so that you can be separated from your possessions.

The truth is that most of the time, offers of a snack, a meal, a gift, or an invitation all are legitimate. If it looks, sounds or feels safe, do it. It's those other circumstances you must look out for.

Encounter Preparedness

As for resistance to you simply being a Westerner, don't take it personally. It all depends what the reputation of travelers is in the area, and the comfort the locals have with Western ways. It's not directed at you, but what you may quite innocently represent. It may be random, like a frowning face staring at you out of a coffee stall as you walk by. Occasionally, it's overt, like being pushed out of the way as locals clamber onto a bus, forcing you to wait for the next one. If you get treated unfairly for simply being you, you're just going to have to roll with it.

Sometimes you might ask for it. Kerry once had to dash to a bank while waiting for a train in a Muslim country. Considering that it was a sweltering ninety degrees out with high humidity, she'd dressed just in shorts, a T-shirt, and sandals. Her bounding body earned glares and rude shouts from men sitting in the shade on the sidewalk; it just wasn't accepted to run around in such revealing garb. Well, she had to endure the heckling because we needed cash but didn't want to miss the train. And they had to put up with what they perceived to be crass behavior from an outsider in their culture.

There are places of real danger, and you will be warned in travel guides and by people you meet coming from that direction.

Encouraging Positivism

In public places, be sensible in what you wear, what you say, and how you move. Read not only for tips on gestures to avoid, but also on proper gestures or actions that promote a harmonious personal encounter or exchange. This is crucial to enjoying favorable interactions with foreigners. If you take some time to acquire cultural knowledge and then practice it confidently, locals will genuinely want to help you. It's the insensitively haughty or ignorant tourist that invites retribution, be it veiled or aggressive.

Money Usage

Wealth Awareness

Thanks to colonial activity of the last 500 years, and more recently, television and tourism, the perception of Western wealth is heavily exported. Be sensitive to the vast differences in wealth, because your level of financial comfort rarely will be achievable by many of the folks you travel among.

Try not to carry more money than you'll need for any two- to four-week period. You don't need the extra bulk. And don't flash it around, or count it in the open. Often, the bills in your money belt total more than the locals around you make in a year.

I learned the hard way. In my impatient enthusiasm once to ride an outrigger canoe on some waves in the South Pacific "Hawaii Five-O"-style, I climbed in the water and paddled out without removing my belt. A wave curled me sideways and washed me under, and soon I was drying strings of travelers checks over a beach fire. While I was standing there damp and feeling sheepish, a local man, kind enough not to laugh at my tipover, noticed my wet AMEX $50s hanging in the smoke. He told me he was paid $1 a day at his job. At that moment I knew what it was like to be the boorish American, let me tell you.

Finding Affordable Lodging

Overnight Planning

I've never once made advance reservations on an adventure trip, except in one tropical nation where it's required of all arriving travelers.

Hotels are everywhere. But beyond airfare, these usually are the big money-gobbler on the road. It is a relief to check in, drop your pack, spread open the tall lacy curtains, collapse on a king-size bed and enjoy the comfy, premium features of a big modern hotel. And at times you need it just to recoup a bit from the rigors of the last travel leg. But unless you're built of gold, being on a long trip calls for you to be on a lean budget. Fortunately there are affordable yet comfortable alternatives.

Lodging Styles

Budget lodging choices in non-Western destinations range from old colonial deluxe hilltop villas, castles or mansions converted to cheap backpacker lodgings, to bed and breakfast-like inns. There are funky bungalow operations, budget hotels or motels, family-run traveler cottages, campgrounds, beach cabanas, college dorm rooms for rent between terms, YMCAs/ YWCAs, hostels, native village dwellings, and friend's homes.

And of course, there's always the free method: pitching your tent in a grassy hollow.

Generally, most areas have popular, proven budget lodgings as well as a few of the equally unpopular odd addresses that give *Psycho*'s Bates Motel a run for its money. Your travel guides and word-of-mouth will help you find rest and avoid a ghastly place. It's actually kind of an adventure not knowing where you'll stay next, and thus exciting when you find a nice place to stay for very little money. While I have a high hassle tolerance, and don't worry a lot in advance that I'll find something acceptable, others like to know ahead of time where they'll be staying. Thankfully, there are choices. I've never found myself in the night's darkness with no option for where to bed down. I guess that's why a tent is a guaranteed fallback.

This basic, budget-preserving $10 room is typical of what's available in hostels, cottages, and beach cabanas. Viti Levu Island, Fiji.

Hostels

There's an economical lodging concept called the youth hostel. Hostels are budget-priced lodging for travelers, with rooms, bunks, showers, a common area, and usually a full cook-it-yourself kitchen with utensils provided. Hostels are a great place for getting the lowdown on local attractions and upcoming events, and to meet other travelers.

Most hostel organizations around the world are better described as people hostels, because any age is welcome. In the U.S., American Youth Hostels (AYH) is the outfit that issues the membership cards necessary to get into International Youth Hostels (IYH) around the world. This card is your "club" card, kind of like a hostel passport that prequalifies you for a bed. There are scores of other hostel organizations around the world now, not affiliated with IYH and not requiring an AYH card, as well as government-run set-ups in your host country. As one of the many budget lodging choices, it's hard to beat a hostel at a few dollars a night.

Hostel Limitations

There can be downsides to hostels. Some are in low-rent locations and may be worn around the edges because they are running on a shoestring. The everyone-does-a-chore job-sharing can go unchecked, leading to discomforts like rank bathrooms. Big hostels in popular places can be crowded and noisy, reminiscent of beery college housing. Further, to stay more than a few nights packed in with a hostel full of equally independent, sensitive, yearning travelers who've journeyed far to get away from it all can be by nature acutely claustrophobic. Yet the price is tempting.

So keep your ears open for word of superior or well-run hostels and support those. They're a big value and they appreciate the money. Write: American Youth Hostels, P.O. Box 37613, Washington, DC 20013 for more information.

Homestays

You also might be interested in homestay organizations. One is Servas, that lets you stay with pre-screened private families or individuals for two nights at a time. Servas's volunteer host households are located in all but a few countries, and there is no charge for you to stay. Once you're accepted as a Servas traveler, you're given a list of Servas members in up to five countries you plan to visit, with their addresses and telephone numbers. At your option, you may call ahead and visit a host. Guests and hosts enjoy a cross-cultural exchange, meals, and fun activities. You pay an annual membership fee of $55, plus a refundable $25 for the list. Write: Servas, 11 John Street, Room 406, New York, NY, 10038.

Extra Features

Overall, there are good lodgings everywhere you go, and wonderful lodgings some places you go. When we've tented, we've found good campgrounds with privacy. When we've stayed in lodgings, we've always found something at least acceptable and often remarkable for the price. And there's always some sort of extra included, like a breakfast, or free movies, or a special view, or hotsprings, or the owner recommending a neat place to visit. And of course, budget lodgings are usually run by the owner and family themselves. Sometimes they'll invite you to eat with them, which can be a fun gathering.

In most instances, a basic bed in a budget lodging such as a cabin, cabana or family-run motel can be found for U.S. $7–15 per night for two people.

Our best low-budget accommodation to date was a combination of simplicity and value, and didn't take any more effort than normal. We didn't find it; a taxi driver took us there when we said we wanted a cheap place to stay. We'd bothered to learn and use a few words of his language to say "low price," "on the water," and "thank you for your help." It was on his island, in a remote place not in the books. We were led to a private campground where only six campers were allowed, on a broad, empty beach, in the shade of palm trees, with a thatched-roof cooking cabana twenty feet from crystal-clear, blue tropical seas. The owner would bring fresh papaya and bananas and hang them off the rafter of the hut. We could snorkel in the lagoon and catch fish and barbecue them or bake them in coconut milk, eating them with steamed breadfruit and sweet potatoes that also were grown in his village's plantation. There was fresh running water from the jungle peaks behind us, brought down and used for the two showers and toilets he'd constructed.

> Traveling by bicycle can put you in some unique places. Two friends were mountain-biking in Jamaica and some locals invited them to camp on a farm, complete with a personal tour the next day. Turns out the tour took them to a two-acre ganja field.

We read, swam the coral reefs, hiked, played cards, ate, and watched magical sunsets. Because we dared to explore, and had a tent, we enjoyed ten days of tropical bliss at U.S. $2.60 per night for two.

That kind of value is still commonly available off the beaten path in non-Western nations. With a little looking you'll find places just like it!

Transport-As-Lodging

One way to save a little on lodging if funds are low is to take night trains, overnight ferries or long-distance night buses where convenient, and sleep on those if you're able.

The Pleasures of Food

Enjoying Choices

Eating ranks as absolutely one of the great joys of an adventure trip. It can be wonderfully tasty—or, when you run across surprises like a tray of pickled whole pig snouts, wonderfully strange. Taking the time to enjoy the pleasures of sampling and dining on local fare is exciting and soul-comforting. Most of the time you'll like what you try.

Mealtime is often the heart of some of the best interchanges with others, both travelers and locals. It generates repartee, exciting conversation and the potential for new travel partners for the next leg of the trip.

It takes many forms. You'll guzzle all manner of concoctions, from standard soft drinks to strange brews. You'll snack from packets of sweets, of nuts or fruit, nibble barbecued kabobs from street vendors, tear open interesting packaged foods from stores, be served fresh, steaming soups and delicacies at sidewalk stalls and restaurant tables, enjoy something hot and delicious off a coal brazier—you name it. The aim is to explore and enjoy the bounty of tastes available to you while avoiding traveler's gastrointestinal discomfort, and anything else unpleasant. Here are some hints for staying healthy.

Ensuring Healthy Liquids

If you can wash your hands with soap before eating, do so. You may want to carry some packets of moist towelettes for face and handcleaning, anyway. Drink only bottled water, and check to be sure it's sealed and not a refilled fake. If there is nothing available and you must use tap water, boil it. Water purification tablets are available but I've never had to use them myself. You also can drink through a portable biofilter straw, or a pump-style water purifier, but again, I've never used the one I carry. As for sodas, juices, beers and wine, the same rules apply. Purchase only sealed bottles, cans or those portable little aseptic juicebox packages.

As for ice, unless you freeze it from a safe source, never use it. It's just the frozen form of the water you don't want to drink. Coffee and tea are fine if the water's been boiled. Fresh-squeezed juice is tempting, but avoid it because it may be mixed with water, or the container it's served into may be contaminated. If you watch it being handsqueezed into a fresh paper cup or something similar, or if you supply the cup, go for it.

Ensuring Healthy Solid Foods

Eat only fruit or vegetables that have been rinsed in clean water and that you yourself can peel or scrape the skin off. This is doubly important due to resident bacteria and the possibility that pesticides are adhered to the skin. Avoid prepared fresh vegetables and fruits, like salads of greens, sliced vegetables, and fruit compotes unless they're prepared in front of you or other travelers are eating them safely. Also stay away from prepared dishes like custards, pastries with sugary goop or meat pastes in them, egg dishes, and cold meat and cheese platters. These all tend to be created in advance, so they sit uncooked and you risk unpleasant results.

Being a dairy-oriented culture, the West is home to cottage cheese, soft cheeses, yogurt, ice cream, butter, and milk. Unfortunately these delights can have a sinister side, too. Are other people eating dairy products? If you're sure the restaurant yogurt poured over morning granola is okay, or the whipped fruit and milk lassi is safe, or the cold foil-wrapped butter squares are fresh, dig in. To decrease the chances of ill health in distant, off-beat zones, vigilant travelers keep away from it all, pasteurized or not.

But I've made exceptions. I've eaten chilled butter on bread, and consumed various refrigerated cheeses packaged in sealed plastic. Feta cheese on a Greek salad has never betrayed me. I've also eaten yogurt because it helps maintain the proper bacterial balance in your stomach. But again, eat only fresh yogurt from sealed containers that are chilled in dairy cases.

"Shelf-stable" or irradiated milk in bags is acceptable, if you're willing to drink sterilized milk. Try the soy milk or rice milk that comes in aseptic packages at grocery stores. It's a good substitute for cow's or goat's milk.

Rice dishes, simple breads, crackers, noodles, pasta, potatoes and all the other similar starch fare are fine if they have been fully cooked or baked. The same applies to any soup or liquid entree that has been boiled.

Remaining are eggs, red meat, pork, fish, shellfish, poultry, and other creatures. You can eat these in any form—skewered, filleted, sliced—as long as they've been freshly cooked, grilled, fried, baked, barbecued or boiled thoroughly. Don't be afraid to examine closely or smell the food.

In the hunger for a certain something, don't neglect to consider whether the source of the meat was healthful. For example, did the fish come from the nearby bay that also is home to an oil refinery? Most of the time you can relax knowing that the food is fine. But in places where people are heavily concentrated be a little more concerned with what you put in your stomach.

Be especially careful of any food caught, raised, or grown downriver from large cities or near any large industrial site. Also, be alert for environmental information on posters, signs or in magazines or newspapers indicating a nearby nuclear power plant, chemical dumping area, refinery, toxic clean-up site, underground nuclear test region, or high pesticide or herbicide spray area.

Picking Restaurants

When judging a restaurant, start by just peeking in. Does it look like a good place? If it looks clean and safe, it usually is. Look for refrigeration equipment, too, because it's a major expense and another sign of the likelihood of quality food. Most of the time, the owner knows a sick patron means a patron who's sharing his woes with other travelers, and keeping business away. So be sure to ask around. If the restaurant's filled with locals or veteran travelers, that's evidence of clean, authentic local fare. If it's recommended by travelers or by a recent edition of your guidebook, go for it.

Cooking Your Own Meals

You easily can cook for yourself where it isn't that cheap to take in every meal at a restaurant. Buy food like noodles, rice, vegetables, and fish at local markets or at neighborhood stores. You can carry a single-burner stove with a butane canister. You can buy these canisters in just about any general merchandise store around the globe. Be sure to finish the canister before you leave a country by airplane, as fuel is forbidden on board. Add a small aluminum frying pan and a boiling pot with lid, some light utensils, a small knife and a few empty film canisters to carry spices, and voila—you can cook anything anywhere.

If you plan to cook at some point during the adventure, rig up your kitchen beforehand. Put together a light, compact packet of cooking gear, so it stows as a unit in your pack or duffel. Then you can use it and store it easily as you go. A light Army surplus mess kit, customized by you, will do the job just fine.

The Experiences of Transportation

Local Transport

Not only is riding local transportation cheap, it's enriching. Traveling shoulder to shoulder with local people lets you meet and talk to them, and lets them have an exchange with you. You see more of the terrain, and get more of a sense for the way locals live and get about. Since they're transiting about as you do, locals often will go out of their way to point out good sights or good places to stay. If you're open, and smile, people just seem to want to help you out and make sure you're going in the right direction. Invariably proud of where they live, they tend to reach out and share their knowledge.

Variety of Methods

No matter where you're traveling, the possibilities on how to get there are endless. In just one day we once rode a three-wheeled scootercab to an airport bus, boarded the turboprop airplane, flew across the country, then hopped on an open-air airport taxi transporter, then rode a bus that

Planes, trains, automobiles...plus ferries, buses, scooters, and oxcarts. You always find transport to take you further. Tokyo, Japan.

rumbled a ways to a ferry. Then—it wasn't even noon yet—we walked onto the ferry that cruised us to a border port, then left the boat into the new country, passed through Customs, and went by taxi and bus to our lodging. It was a major transit day with nothing else planned, but it illustrates the variety of overseas commuting. We've ridden in horse-drawn carriages, on bicycles and scooters, motorboats, on trains, long-haul buses, canoes, "African Queen"-style, smoke-belching ferryboats, gondolas, and pedicabs. A hot air balloon would be fun, too. Maybe next time.

Low-Cost Transport

Getting around by public transportation generally is cheap and easy. There is usually a boat, train, local plane, or bus going where you are. It isn't always comfortable, and occasionally it's brutal. You can always elevate to another level of comfort based on a bad previous experience. Also, as an alternative to (or instead of) public transportation you can hitchhike.

While I haven't thumbed much, we've had some great rides. One was from a friendly New Zealander who turned out to be a off-duty police officer on his Christmas holiday. He loaded us and our packs into his car, which he'd already crammed with gifts, and drove us across the south island of New Zealand on an all-day ride, complete with a stop for a jump in a thermal hot springs. We shared a bag of fresh-picked cherries before he dropped us off in Christchurch at our lodging. We've been more inclined to hitchhike in countries where English is common than in countries where we can't communicate with the driver, but you might be more open to it—especially if you speak a bit of the foreign language.

Take a few moments with the driver to agree on your destination and what time you want to get there. Look the driver in the eyes, and make sure they look at you. If he slurs his words, or if you feel unsure, or if you see alcohol, drugs, or weapons, don't get in. Open and leave open the car or truck door before loading your pack in the back, so they're less able to drive off with it. Or, climb in and have them load it.

Renting Cars

Renting a car is expensive, so if you have coupons or can share a car with others, or hire from a rent-a-wreck kind of operation, it gets cheaper. The benefit is total freedom to roam where you will, and it may be worth the expense. You also can sleep in the car and save on lodging. Or, if you have a tent, your car will get you to an out-of-the-way place where you can camp for the night, avoiding the fees of a dedicated car campground.

Buying Cars

Another alternative is to buy a used car or used motorcycle, drive it while exploring, then sell it. This way your transportation is free except for gas. This is common practice in Australia, where taking a beat-up station wagon several thousand miles from Sydney to Perth or Melbourne to Darwin isn't too cost-effective for a resident to do. They still have to head all those thousand miles back home. But being a traveler heading in one direction with time on your hands, you can do these or similar trips. We've heard many stories of people traveling across Australia by buying a station wagon or van for transport and for sleeping in, driving for a couple of months, then selling it at that trip leg's end for more than they bought it.

You can do this all over the world, but you must register yourself as the owner or risk fines. You will have to pay some registration fees, but registering a car makes it easier to sell to the next person.

Carnets

Certain countries that don't see a lot of traveling Westerners ask your vehicle to have a passport as well as you, whether you are renting the car or motorcycle or have bought it. This is generally referred to as a carnet (from the French word for passbook). It's more than simply carrying a driver's license. This collection of paperwork may include insurance papers, stamped rental papers, temporary import certificate, official ownership documents, a personal guarantee bond to return the vehicle to the rental agency, and so on. The carnet calms country officials. They don't want you to sell your vehicle in their country "off the market" which means they're unable to collect a tax or fee. Also, an incomplete carnet allows them to impound your vehicle until they choose to release it.

AAA can guide you on details before you depart, as can the rental agency or dealership where you're traveling. Or phone the U.S. Embassy or Consulate in the region.

Gringos-for-lunch scam: a friend and his wife were swarmed by fifty taxi drivers as the two emerged from Acapulco's airport baggage claim. Tired, and anxious to be at their hotel, they were overwhelmed, swept into a cab, and hustled off for a costly ride. Lesson: always set the fare in advance.

Staying In Touch On The Road 8

In Kalimantan (Borneo), jungle travelers tie arrangements of leaves onto sticks as news, so others following can read updates as they pass by.

▲▼▲▼▲▼▲▼▲▼▲▼▲▼▲▼▲▼▲▼▲▼▲▼▲▼▲

A brutal Spanish general hunting gold in the 1500s in South America, and captured by native tribesmen, was forced to drink a molten bowlful.

▲▼▲▼▲▼▲▼▲▼▲▼▲▼▲▼▲▼▲▼▲▼▲▼▲▼▲

Asia's football-sized durian fruit smells like a warm outhouse. But fans swear the sweet custard inside tastes like heaven.

You're exploring. You're in a completely unusual travel reality now, and world news may have slimmed to a trickle. (Some places don't have satellite dishes, for example. In some places, people aren't yet sure what a satellite is.) No matter how in touch you need to be, here's where to find world news. We'll also discuss using mail—both the postal kind and the electronic kind—and other methods for ensuring you receive news from home. Then you can go right back to your hammock with a cool drink and a suspenseful paperback.

All the News that Fits

The Dilemma of News Consumption

Trying to keep up with what is going on around the world while you're worlds away is an adventure in itself. In my experience, it hasn't been easy to get used to less access to news. Feeling out of touch has led me to realize that at home I become hooked on current information. Disconnecting from it isn't easy.

Travel also has revealed that mainstream news shapes a range of misconceptions about places overemphasizing the bad or the good. But no image or sequence of words and images can replace the excitement of being there live. Places have their own wonder. People and cultures have their own masterful presence that TV can't fully reveal.

As for news on the road, it's like anywhere: the world's events happen in real time, constantly and in the present. And in the West we're used to having it ladled over us, all the news we want right now, or "at eleven."

But on the road in non-Western locations, current global news is harder to find. While traveling in populated areas, you might hear of events as they happen, such as seeing it on the TV news or in the day's paper. But just as often, you're behind the times, seeing them from the past. For example, you might come into a city from a spell in the wild to find a newsstand, fruit stand, or gas station carrying only battered, six week old *Time* magazines, and not in English. You glance at the pictures and realize there is a world out there, and you forgot about it. And you feel caught in the "where am I?" torpor, with the impression that time has marched right past you.

The flip side is that some travelers don't want to know what's

Take advantage of modern services when touring cities. They're easier to call home from, do banking in, and find world news. Hong Kong.

happening. Traveling in far-away places can put you in a pleasing reality of your own, where time stretches out and sets you adrift, having left home and dropped out of current events. Yacht passengers know this syndrome, and many find it a very enjoyable way of life. Severed from the mainland, they seldom feel the need to stay updated on news.

In the midst of adventure it can be downright annoying to bump into the latest news, and you may feel as if your travel dream has been interrupted. It can make you wonder why news was so important to you, and just how it affected your life so much. If you're out for a good while, your travel experiences and local or regional issues fill your plate. Off-beat adventure travel can put you in the company of locals who aren't operating in this century. Some people live, eat, and sleep in a mindset that revolves around habits or traditions unaffected by world events. As you hang out for a while and adopt local ways, you yourself may go back in time. Current events from the other side of the globe can seem alien and futuristic when you're immersed in much simpler cultures than those of the Western world.

News Sources

Fortunately, if you're interested, you can find all the news you need. You'll never be far from the daily *International Herald-Tribune*, for example, a global joint-venture newspaper of the *New York Times* and *Washington Post*. Look at newsstands and hotel gift shops, airports, and train stations. International editions of *Time*, *Newsweek*, and the *Wall Street Journal* are available at newsstands too. You'll see TV and hear radio programs like the BBC World Service and Voice of America. Fellow travelers will also provide you with their own colorful news and opinions.

Another way to get caught up is to head to a branch of the United States Information Service (USIS). A unit of the Department of State that provides a library, films, and news, the USIS also is a good place to hang your hat for a few hours and scan some daily papers, meet other travelers, or hook up with locals who may want to show you around or practice their English.

The Reassurance of Mail

Sending and Receiving

Sending mail feels great, and getting mail is wonderful.

If you'll be on the go and won't have a fixed address for your friends or family to write to, leave them a copy of your itinerary and have them contact you at the main post offices of the major cities you'll be passing through. Always have them send letters first class airmail—not second, third or fourth class or "Regular" or "Surface" mail. Those classes typically mean ship and truck and train instead of air, and can take several weeks.

Mail Hold

Poste Restante is a French phrase for "held mail." The main post offices of cities in most countries will hold mail in your name, as long as those who write you label the envelopes "Poste Restante" in big letters. Some countries use different phrases for this purpose, so be sure to check your guidebook. Alternatively, American Express will hold your mail for thirty days if you're a member. We've used AMEX exclusively for receiving and holding all our mail on all our trips.

Postcards, letters, stamps, mailboxes, and post offices are used the world over. But avoid mailboxes when mailing letters or smaller packages home, if possible. Instead, take all mail to the main post office yourself, and always ask that your stamps are franked (stamped or canceled) in front of you. Otherwise, those clean stamps could be tempting to someone handling the mail and you might literally be ripped off, your precious news dumped away.

Notify everyone who'll be writing you to capitalize your last name on the envelope and underline it, giving you a better chance of receiving it. .

For fun, consider writing a letter and faxing it home. It costs a bit more, but it will get there fast. Look for fax signs in business districts of towns or at large hotels.

Mail Shipping

Sometimes you may need to ship certain items home. If your travel book says local mail sometimes is unreliable, take bigger or more valuable packages directly to an air courier service like DHL or the cargo wing of a reputable international airline. You also might want to call the U.S. embassy or consulate and ask what they recommend.

Ship jewelry, film negatives, gifts, and other important items using reputable firms in larger cities. You can trust the big companies like DHL, Federal Express, Airborne, and the cargo wings of major international airlines. It's worth carrying your special items for a while longer until you get to a city with an international airport, rather than putting them in the rural mail stream from some remote country village and hoping they eventually arrive home in one piece.

If you'll be shipping perishable goods like food or agricultural items, your best chance of successful delivery is from big cities with an international airport. It may be best to buy the items when departing for home, or when you know they can be airshipped immediately. Fresh goods need to be transported quickly by air, so if you buy from a reputable store that ships fresh purchases frequently, you can feel confident. Alternatively, you may want to actually carry the goods yourself.

Almost all fresh items have to go through U.S. Customs, so ask the merchant or the airline cargo outfit about any restrictions. You also can call the embassy or consulate at your departing city. Or, send for the "Know Before You Go" Customs checklist mentioned previously.

News travels at strange speeds. While a friend was traveling in Sumatra, an earthquake there made headlines in the world's press. Her parents, 12,000 miles away in the U.S., hung by the phone waiting for news she was safe. But it took a week before she herself heard the news, though it had happened just a few hundred miles south.

Electronic Communication

Telephones

In the U.S. you can make a phone call from a payphone in a jetliner and pay with a quick swipe of a credit card.

Outside the U.S., phone systems tend to be much more rudimentary. You will find phones just about everywhere you go, but they may not be easy to use or even easy to understand how to use.

Some places have odd, must-buy-token-first arrangements, indecipherable how-to symbols on the phone, or poor connections, which either will be charming or aggravating, depending on your sense of humor that day. Your best bet is to take care of telecommunication needs when passing through large cities, as they typically have the country's best phone equipment. Go to the post, telephone and telegraph office (PTT or similar) to place your call. Operators there usually speak English.

Major phone companies in the U.S. offer international calling cards that are pretty nifty. You punch in a few numbers from a phone anywhere on the globe, and reach an English-speaking international operator who'll put you through to the party you're calling. Call AT&T, Sprint or MCI for further details. Remember, there may be several hours—or even a full day—between you and the person you're calling. Keep this in mind on important days like birthdays and holidays. Check a time zone map before placing an overseas call.

Portable Computers

A portable computer is like a fine camera—convenient, but delicate. If you're considering taking a laptop computer on your trip, be sure you'll really use it. They're still expensive and weigh several pounds. They have limited battery life, and accessories like batteries weigh extra. Recharging a computer requires using electrical outlets that may not be available or may be the wrong shape or voltage. And protecting your computer from the elements, the rigors of travel, and theft will be an ongoing task.

But a computer may be worth bringing for the convenience it provides. You can transmit and receive documents immediately, via phone lines or electronic networks. An alternative is to rent or borrow computers at hotels, businesses, or schools, carrying floppy disks with you.

Electronic Mail

It's now possible to send and receive electronic mail from many foreign destinations. You can go to a local university, government building, hotel, or computer center and locally log on to the Internet. There you can open, read, and send e-mail messages. You might consider approaching a multinational company's offices in a major city on your route and borrowing one of their personal computers to access with. Also, you might carry a personal digital assistant (PDA), such as an Apple Newton, which allows sending and receiving files and faxes electronically or by phone. Consumer reports have been positive on PDAs, especially as the technology and design improves.

Cellular Phones

Most travelers either want to stay in touch or stay undisturbed. Having a cellular phone lets you do both at the flick of a switch. The drawback is that cellular technology—which requires microwave dishes to handle phone traffic in dedicated local cellular sites—is basically non-existent in sparsely populated or remote areas. This type of technology is evolving at the, ahem, speed of light. Ask a major provider, like AT&T, Sprint, or MCI what they offer where you're going, and maybe a cellular phone will work for you. A hundred years from now, you'll probably be able to buy a two-way worldwide voice-dialing wristphone with a tiny color viewscreen for fifty cents. Until then, enjoy the peace and quiet.

Global Positioning System

If you're planning to *really* push the envelope on second-generation travel, a GPS locator may be of interest.

If you're overland trekking across little-known regions like north-central Asia, the interior of equatorial Africa or South America, or perhaps kayaking or sailing for a long time in rarely visited tropical islands, you could get lost. Weather and unfamiliar terrain may disorient you when you're many weeks from civilization or known landmarks.

Navigation is a science and an art, and largely dependent on your maps, itinerary, experience, and accuracy. Large, expensive GPS systems are common in cross-country hauling, ocean shipping, fishing, and yachting. For a few hundred dollars, you can buy a scaled-down unit the size of a deck of cards that digitally displays your latitude, longitude, and altitude off orbiting satellites. It's the ultimate compass to keep you on track. Look in the back of hunting or backpacking magazines for advertisements, or you can order from Gander Mountain Outfitters, (800) 558-9410.

Taking time to travel gives you leisure to read, write, compose, and paint. Kerry records the day's events. Ubud, island of Bali, Indonesia.

The Pleasures of Reading

Finding Books

Part of the luxury of extended travel is the freedom to really savor leisure activities like reading. Avid readers should take a couple of paperbacks to read when they first leave on a trip, but that's it. Any more is heavy and unnecessary, as there are bookstores with books in English almost everywhere travelers go. Check near bus and train stations and near shopping markets. You can buy and read your paperbacks en route, then sell or give them away. You'll read a lot of interesting books when you trade with others, too.

Books As Cash

If you're looking for a little extra cash, and heading to a remote or undeveloped country with some room when you take off, bring a few extra paperbacks—the kind you buy at garage sales for twenty-five cents. English paperbacks go for $2–4 per title in traveler's enclaves, and you can make some extra pocket money along the way. That's a nights lodging or a day of meals in some places.

Diversions On The Road 9

A woven straw Panama hat made in Panama isn't a true "Panama." Those come from Ecuador.

▲▼▲▼▲▼▲▼▲▼▲▼▲▼▲▼▲▼▲▼▲▼▲▼▲

Golf attracts tourists, but maintaining golf courses isn't cheap, so some tropical islands have grass airstrips that double as fairways.

▲▼▲▼▲▼▲▼▲▼▲▼▲▼▲▼▲▼▲▼▲▼▲▼▲

Australians put up the Christmas tree, hang the ornaments, string the lights, and wait for Santa. In their shorts, flip flops, and 90 degree weather.

Remember all that money you saved up? It's now time to spend it! Read on for ways to use it wisely, so you can get more out of your precious funds. This section includes advice on how to shop, when to pay, how to pay, and when to walk away and go take some pictures instead. Plus, tips on adding intensified mini-adventures onto the big one you're having. Also, advice on how to find animals and nature sites to enjoy. Finally, ways to make more money through on-the-road jobs, then traveling back to the beginning of this paragraph.

Shopping, Negotiating, and Buying

Market Techniques

What ranks as one of the great adventures of travel? Shopping! Not only is it fun to snoop out deals, but bargaining with good-natured local vendors often ends with handshakes and laughter. And there is an added pleasure if that vendor actually crafted the item him- or herself.

Depending on where you are, the posted price may have nothing to do with what you eventually pay and you'll be expected to negotiate. Sometimes these encounters offer the finest drama, complete with bluff openings, smiles, lower offers, pouts, and feigned incredulity that you'd even try to go so low, frowns, concession, a shout, arms raised with palms open—and suddenly a deal is struck. In other places the posted price is the final price, and there is no room for debate.

Obviously, each of us has our own idea about worth, and what comprises value, and what suits our fancy. Yet we all have the same opinion about being taken. To help prevent this from happening, we've included some advice on how to protect your funds in any purchase— from a bar of soap to a bus fare to a night's lodgings to a beautiful silk blouse.

Local Knowledge

You've made some big financial decisions and sacrifices to even be on this trip in the first place. Accordingly, once on your adventure, you'll know how to focus on economy and buy selectively. Incidental purchases like snacks, postcards, fruit, film, matches, and meals are easy. But what about those things you spend big money on?

The best way to ensure paying a fair price for what you buy is to take a little time to learn about the buying power of the local currency. Find out what the working daily wage is. Many artists who don't sell their own work receive just a small percentage per piece. Ask yourself if the price is more or less than you'd pay at home.

Know what a dollar gets you locally. Determine if paying with a traveler's check buys more than paying in the national coin. Ask other travelers what they paid for the things they're carrying. Watch some transactions between locals. What bills are being passing back and forth? What change is given? Are buyers paying the posted price? Are they haggling? Think to yourself what you'd be willing to pay. If you feel the that price of a particular item is fair, pay it.

You should expect to pay more than locals, but don't contribute to the practice of exorbitant markups by always shelling out top dollar.

Bargaining Skills

Getting a good price will take confident bargaining skills. Using local negotiating tactics lets you feel sure you're paying no more than you need to. If negotiating is the norm, locals prefer the game and you can embarrass them by not bargaining.

To be taken seriously, you have to be willing to walk away. That's because your price comfort zone may be too low for the merchant at that moment; perhaps he or she is doing some decent business and can afford not to budge on their price.

Know and use the "I'll come back later, maybe" dodge, in their language. Know the words for "How much?," "Too expensive," "Tomorrow," and "I can only pay ___."

Consider waiting until the end of the day to make an offer on something, and then stall a bit at closing time. They may be more anxious to close the day with a decent sale. If the item you're looking at is widely available you can expect to get farther with the merchant. They know their item is common and that you can simply walk to the next dealer if they won't play ball. This way, they may be more inclined to meet your price.

We once needed three separate visits to get the price we thought was fair for two paintings in Bali. It was the difference between $60 and $30—a lot to a budget traveler—and we eventually got a price we were happy with. So be willing to be patient and take this kind of time for something you really want.

Shops and markets in lesser-developed economies are where the bargains live. Some merchants take offense if you don't negotiate!

Money Saving Tips

Some other possibilities are to go in with another traveler and get a two-for-one deal. Or pay a higher price on a spendier item but insist that the sale include some accessory for free, like a matching bracelet or belt or pair of sandals to go with that skirt and blouse. Or if you've made a local friend you trust, tell them what you want and let them buy it for you. He or she is an insider, and is intimately familiar with local selling practices.

Fair Attitude

Say you join friends for a morning in an Arab central *souq* to shop, and you start bargaining with the merchant for a fluffy, soft sheepskin rug. If you don't get the price you want, don't get steamed. You're free to leave and browse at the next sheepskin stall, while this guy has to sit surrounded by piles of the slightly fragrant things, hawking the stuff from dawn to dusk. Remember how lucky you are to be traveling. Be a respectful guest on their turf.

Don't begin to bargain seriously with someone unless you really want the item. After a successful haggling session you're obligated to buy. If it's a fair price and you don't make a purchase, you make an enemy of someone who resents your head games. Plus you might have taken them away from more willing customers. Play fair and make it easy for the next traveler.

Paying for Items

Pay with cash or traveler's checks for most items. Use a credit card when you think you might need to dispute or cancel the transaction if the item is faulty. A good example where this might come in handy is electronics. If a new camera or Walkman-style radio you buy has counterfeit components, jams up the day after you buy it, and the seller refuses to take it back; or if an in-country flight costing $200 is canceled— you'll be glad you charged it.

Keep track which traveler's checks you write, and for what. Get a receipt for purchases you'll be bringing home, so Customs personnel in the country you're in will see it's not being smuggled out. Also, a proof of purchase assures you don't get slapped with unnecessary duty by U.S. Customs on your return.

Preventing Errors

When paying with a credit card, never lose sight of it. A wily merchant, figuring you're just passing through, may walk into the back office and process a second receipt, and fill it in with a bogus purchase. It appears on your bill at home long after you've left the country, he gets paid, and you're the loser. It's difficult to prove you didn't make the purchase if there's another legitimate one from the same store on the same day.

If a merchant is still using old free-floating carbons in their credit blanks, insist on being given the carbon to tear up into little pieces. It can be used to duplicate receipts if you don't.

Gifts for Home

Gifts cost money that can eat into your travel budget in a major way, so bring extra money for them. You can ship home what you can't carry. Air shipping takes days, and boat shipping, though much cheaper, takes many weeks or months.

Before you buy something for yourself, ask if you really can see yourself liking that life-size brocade orange wood flamingo for years to come. Kerry and I think we buy selectively, yet we still have managed to collect a couple of duds over the years.

Capturing Great Moments

Photography

Pictures can bring home your best memories. A penguin skimming the pink waves of a Greek sunset. The liquid luster of the dark eyes of an Algerian village girl. A yellow frog with red spots sitting on a green banana leaf in Honduras.

After years of traveling I have one major regret. That is that I didn't take many photos while traveling until after I met Kerry, who is a photographer. Shooting was never a big deal to me. But I've come around to really appreciate the effort we now make.

Still photography is one of the best ways to capture and bring home memories of your trip for yourself, for your children if you have or plan to have them, and for your friends. The kind of traveling we're talking about is special, and deserves to be well-documented.

Photography lets you catalogue the adventures you have, the friends you made, the awesome places you saw. After you get home you'll want to remember what it all felt like. And others will want to see what you did. Being able to thumb through a photo album or view slides makes it possible. Plus, when you get the hankering to leave again and you can't, and the old soul needs a little reminding of the joys of travel, a look through trip photos can give it a boost.

Look at the possibility of selling some of your photos as stock photography. Or mounting them on greeting cards and selling them for extra income, as a friend of mine has done. Enlarging and mounting some choice shots is a great way to liven up your work area. And a photo can make an exciting holiday card.

Equipment Choices

As for selection, if you know what you're doing take the best equipment you can, including a lightweight, collapsible tripod. Review all your accessories and take what you need, considering weight in your decision. Do you really need a third lens when two will do?

If you're more of a "stop 'n' snap" shooter, take the auto-everything type camera. There are some fine affordable cameras available these days. Get one with a telephoto lens and a fill-flash, for bringing landscapes closer and to add light to shaded subjects. They give great results even though they aren't designed for much creativity.

Protect your gear from the elements and the rigors of travel. If your camera gets damaged, a look inside the instruction manual will get you a list of repair locations around the world. Or stick your head in a camera shop. They may know a local who works on your brand if the official repair facility is a long ways off.

Some new cameras are weatherized, with a special shell and gasket to help the camera resist water and dirt. Prices are dropping on these cameras, so they may be worth a look.

Film Use and Processing

You could take good gear (a 35 mm SLR-type camera) and learn as you go, but that would require developing along the way in order to check your progress. This isn't a bad idea, as photo developing outside the U.S. often can be cheaper, especially in Third World locations. But you may discover that on a long trip you don't want to spend energy on trial-and-error photography. With a little work you can get fantastic shots.

A friend's camera stopped working in Indonesia, and she mentioned it to a traveler. Incredibly, the traveler's husband repaired cameras. He agreed to fix it, and to return it a few days later in the next town. Illness and sudden travel changes led to a mix-up. It was three months later, 2,000 miles away in Thailand, that they ran into each other in Bangkok. He had her fixed camera.

Shoot as much as you can early and late in the day to get good light and contrasts, and to minimize glare.

Take a lead-lined bag for protecting your exposed film from light and radiation. Airport security booths and other such devices cannot always be relied upon as safe for film, no matter what the sign or the guard says. Always try to carry your gear and film through these security checks by hand.

Film, supplies, accessories, and developing services are readily available just about everywhere. This usually includes same-day developing services, though these facilities tend to be located in large cities or highly touristed areas.

Some countries include the cost of developing in the purchase price of the film. If you'll be doing a lot of shooting but really need to cut corners, here's a cost-saving tip. Ask a fellow traveler/photographer who's been to a country you're heading to if developing is included in the price of film. If it is, and you have some used-up rolls, hold off on developing your already-shot film until you get to that country. They might consider your film prepaid for developing. You also might buy some film before you arrive in the country, then shoot it in that country and have it developed there before you leave.

Recording Your Impressions

Personal Journal

Along with taking photographs, there are mental and emotional impressions you'll want to remember. A fine way to record thoughts and feelings is to keep a personal journal and jot in it when you're inspired. Kerry kept one on our last trip and included colored pencil drawings. Now it's a great treasure, a period piece from a fun time in her life. Your letters home can become your personal journal, combining news with impressions. To save postage and time, designate someone at home to photocopy and distribute your letters to your friends and family.

If you write infrequent but highly detailed letters, photocopy the good ones before mailing them. Sometimes mail doesn't make it home, and you'll be glad to have a full record of your trip to read later.

Be sure to write close to the fact. Your writing and thoughts will be fresher, truer, more alive if you record them as soon as possible. If you wait a week or more after an event it will become a little hazy, and you'll spend valuable time and energy playing catch-up. For better reading later, get it on paper as soon as it happens.

You can have people you meet write in your journal too, or sign their names and addresses.

Tape Recordings

Another fun way to remember your trip is to carry a little handheld microcassette dictaphone to narrate events and record sounds. Months or years later, listening to conversations on trains, or to the creaking of old wooden wagonwheels on a rocky road, or to the call of jungle birds can take you in an instant back to the places you visited.

Video Cameras

Naturally, this brings us to the moving image. The proliferation of light, affordable handheld video cameras make using one a fun alternative. You get the ability to portray movement and activities in their entirety, plus sound, the ability to erase what you don't want, and an archive from which to edit custom versions of travel highlights. Ask your dealer whether you can get blank recording tape on the road in the same size and format your videocamera accepts. If not, you'll have to carry your own. Plan to shoot on batteries only. If you can handle a few extra ounces, carry back-up batteries. Regardless, you should be able to find fresh ones wherever you are, although in remote places batteries tend to hang around on racks for quite awhile and can be weak from the start.

Some videocameras have special lightweight, weather-resistant carry cases, helping to protect them from the elements.

The downside to videocameras is that the best light ones are like the best 35 mm SLR cameras: still pretty expensive, and fragile due to a lot of plastic components. They have moisture- and temperature-sensitive electronic parts that are not cheap to repair. Water, dust, sand, humidity and the jostles of the road all can cause them to seize up. Further, videotape can't offer the versatile frame composition, texturing, and rich film color results that a still film camera can. And then there's the viewing decision: is it better to watch color slides shot on film viewed up big on a wall or screen, or tape rolling on a smaller TV or monitor? Being a fundamentally different tool than a still camera, it's simply a matter of personal choice. Carrying both a camera and a videocamera is the best solution if you can afford it. But that means more weight, so do what you like. You could always ship home the one you use less of if you got tired of carrying both.

Scrapbook Mementos

Along with pictures, slides, videotapes, and recorded sound, there are scrapbook mementos. Save those train ticket stubs, local maps, leaves or dried flowers, handwritten notes, beer coasters, package labels, event posters, postcards, small menus, and all the other little items you run into, and mail them home when you've collected a batch. They're really fun to assemble later in a scrapbook to go along with your photos. They add real flavor to your memories, and, like the visa stamps in your passport, they're genuine proof of your adventure.

Special Adventures

Adventure Mini-Trips

You're likely familiar with adventure travel tours like photo safaris or rafting down the Zambezi River. Other trips include kayaking or trout fishing in New Zealand, with a little bungee jumping thrown in. Or how about sailing and snorkeling for a few days in the Maldives, near India. Just about every place on the planet offers something fun and adventurous to do. Expensive? Yes—if you only have two or three weeks off from work. Adventure travel companies will take you to these exotic locations for a sizable fee. Of course, it usually includes your airfare, lodging, meals, and transit fees so you don't have to deal with arranging those kinds of details.

But if you've arrived someplace of your own volition, you can enjoy those same adventures yourself for a fraction of the cost.

Often, the U.S. operators of these sorts of fun adventures have local offices in the countries where they do business. Sometimes the U.S. operator rents the services of an independent travel outfit to handle the arriving groups. Either way, whether it's a branch of the U.S. operator or a local independent, most usually take walk-in participants.

Types of Mini-Adventures

Business may or may not be hopping, and depending on the season you can step right in and pay local prices and share in the adventure. It could be as simple as riding a camel for an afternoon somewhere in the Middle East. Or a more involved affair, like a light-impact eco-tour in South America or two-week guided trek in the Himalayas. Suffice it to say that if it's being done somewhere by adventure trippers as a part of a prepaid, all-inclusive trip, you probably can join in at the source.

Some of these adventures you'll set up yourself, like arranging to fly by missionary plane to the interior of Kalimantan (Borneo), and hiking and canoeing out with native Dayak guides. Some involve piggybacking onto other people's trips, like walking over to a hotel and joining the all-day lake cruise, luncheon, and "shore-explore" excursion arranged primarily for guests. Others are pieced together, like arriving somewhere by lazy inter-island ferry instead of pricy private turboprop, then renting motorcycles or a small sailboat for a few days and exploring the same remote stretches of an island favored by big-name adventure travel firms.

Or do it straight. Shell out the bucks and join the full-blown, twelve-day adventure group as it heads into the bush. You'll still save money on the trip by getting to the point of departure yourself. You'll be splurging for the experience and the marvelous bonus of memories it will give your overall trip, then dropping back down to budget levels afterwards and moving on. It's a fun way to meet people. But the best part is that you get to keep traveling while the others have to get back on the jet home. And boy will they wish they were you.

Day Adventures

You also can do smaller-sized adventures to spice up the trip while preserving your travel funds. We once left the beaches behind and spent a great day on a special trip to a ruin in the Yucatan being regaled by an incredible half-Mayan, half-Dutch guide and raconteur named Pinky. Another time, we detoured from a regional town and were led by a Burmese guide on a three-day hike into some of the colorfully dressed, animist, opium-puffing hill tribes of North Thailand.

Even if you're going to skip the rush of an intensified adventure-within-your-adventure, you'll still find yourself regularly enjoying the benefit of sheer economical off-the-beaten-path budget travel. Like heading by twenty-five cent bus from your $4 cabana to the tropical tip of some peninsula and renting a $2 sailboard for an hour of breezy floating, followed by a $1 market-bought lunch and a nap under a palm tree. It's a beachy blue day, just like on the postcards, that costs you $7.25. In fact, it's the same kind of day the adventure group is enjoying up the coast a ways, except that while their sailboards are free, their rooms cost $95.

Finding Animals

Where to Look

No matter where in the world you find yourself, you'll be able to pursue animals. The idea is for them not to pursue you.

Unfortunately, as more of the world becomes less wild, the chances of seeing an animal in its natural state are decreasing. Your risk of getting harmed, in a sad way, is decreasing. But it isn't all gloom. In the realm of wildlife, many nations are quite conscious of the animal kingdom and take a protective national stance. Travelers are encouraged to witness animals in the wild, to enjoy them and also to see that even the most ferocious are still at our mercy. This forward-looking attitude can help you come home with a greater appreciation of nature's fragility. These countries further protect animals with vast reserves, parks, and wilderness areas. In other countries it's a travesty. There, wild animals are seen as irrelevant or as obstacles to development, or economic conditions make them more valuable as dinner or to hang on a wall or to dissect and smuggle out as ashtrays or aphrodisiacs.

Types of Animals

There are places where animals really stand out, such as in Africa,

Pick a base, then do area day trips to see animals and other sights. You see more, rush less. Then, move to your next base. Tanzania.

Eastern Russia, Alaska, tropical rainforests, the Galapagos Islands, and so on. Elsewhere, looking for and finding animals other than in enclosed or dedicated areas will take some determination, but you can do it. You will find beautiful birds, stunning mammals, slinky reptiles and more. You can go to special preserves, like the sidetrip we once made to a Malaysian farm that raises butterflies and moths for zoos and collectors. Your travel guidebook will describe these sites and the chances for seeing wildlife there. A local person or area expert leading the way can improve the odds.

As for the dangers of certain animals, try to get a handle on which ones to avoid. Your travel books should have some tips. The potential for lethal danger varies around the globe. On land, watch for certain furry animals big and small, and various bats, snakes, insects and spiders. In the sea, keep an eye out for sharks, barracuda, moray eels, sea snakes, some jellyfish, or venom-quilled fish or shellfish. In fresh water be aware of crocs and 'gators, piranha, and strange waterborne things like insects and bacteria that can get nasty if they get inside you.

Know what lives where and what attracts them, and you'll do just fine as you go about your explorations. Travel guidebooks and information at the kiosks of national parks will help you stay safe.

Finally, don't buy any trinket or gift made with animal parts. Doing so contributes to the practice of killing animals for their anatomy, which is illegal in many countries.

Finding Plants

Where to Look

Searching for beautiful or unique plants, trees, and flowers will be hindered by the same force affecting animals: man. Overpopulation, overgrazing, excessively applied artificial fertilizers, herbicides, and pesticides, industrial blight, irrigation, air and water pollution, and deforestation all increasingly plague many otherwise plant-rich parts of the planet. Still, as in the case of animals, you will be amazed by what you can find. Many botanical gardens, nature preserves, rainforest parks, and zoos feature native plants and are easy to get to. When trekking in the wild, a guide or knowledgeable person can help locate that evasive flora specimen.

Possible dangers include thorned species and those with toxins on their leaves. Be careful of any samples offered for tasting, or of teas or salads prepared with wild gathered greens. Also avoid mushrooms with which you aren't familiar.

Funding Travel through Working

Travel Hiatus

You might be low on funds, or perhaps just want to have a home base for a few weeks or months while you build up your savings again. Ideally, you're traveling strictly to travel. But some folks on longer trips like to break up life on the road with a little work. This makes them feel better about traveling for long periods of time. Or, they want to work (or volunteer) to gain experience, get to know an area, or to help out someone they've met or a cause they care about. No matter the motivation, it's nice simply to add some money to the budget.

You may well gain experience that helps advance your career when you return home, along with getting paid for your labors while you're there.

Types of Jobs

There are two types of jobs you can have on the road: official and unofficial. It's a distinction that's important, because it may be illegal to work as an alien unless you have official sanction. You should be prepared to face the consequences—sometimes as extreme as jail or deportation—if caught.

Job hunting for official positions is much like in the U.S. Scan newspapers, visit temporary employment agencies, read bulletin boards at stores, post offices, or where you're staying, and approach businesses. Also, contact embassies, consulates, schools, universities, and cultural institutions. Ask around.

Before applying you may have to get a letter or card that says it is legal for you to work. Play honestly with the federal government if you plan to work at any job for more than six months, because you usually will get noticed.

Unofficial jobs are more short-term, ranging from a week to two months, and don't impede your traveling so much. They can expose you to the authorities, too, but less easily than official jobs. They tend to be "cash and carry" positions like picking fruit, helping out on a farm, doing repair or cleaning, serving food, or assisting at a restaurant. You can make some quick money, then move on.

If you see an opportunity, go for it. I met a German guy once who was designing and lettering beautiful, colorful tropical T-shirts for a few weeks at $5 a shirt, several shirts per day, at an Indian clothing store in Fiji. He got the job by walking in and telling them he had done it before—which wasn't true—but it did help that he drew well. Look for notices on hostel bulletin boards; train, bus, and airport kiosks; and at boat docks and yacht clubs. Or offer to do some work for someone in exchange for lodging or meals.

Work can be play. We met a couple from France who saw a notice at a pier for crew on board a yacht sailing the islands of the West Pacific for two months. They interviewed with the skipper and without any experience got the jobs and sailed away into the sunset.

For more information on overseas jobs and volunteer opportunities, see the bibliography.

Personal Matters On The Road 10

Most intact indigenous tribes globally who don't eat processed food, don't eat refined sugar, and don't use toothbrushes, have the world's best teeth.

▲▼▲▼▲▼▲▼▲▼▲▼▲▼▲▼▲▼▲▼▲▼▲▼▲

Early travelers to the Middle East and North Africa reported sultans with as many as 200 concubines in their harems.

▲▼▲▼▲▼▲▼▲▼▲▼▲▼▲▼▲▼▲▼▲▼▲▼▲

Balinese dancers go into trances and attempt to stab sharp-bladed "kris" knives into their sides, to test their faith. Typically, they can't.

You'll be running into fascinating people on your trip. Exotic-looking people. Sometimes, attractive personalities with desirable features. This section includes more on negotiating all the potential interpersonal paths, sweet or perilous, whether you're single or not. This is followed by ideas for staying fit and sprinkling exercise into your regular travel excursions. Lastly, comments on what you, as a Western traveler, are bringing to the little-known place you visit. Just a small wake-up call, for making sure you can truly relax inside your adventurous traveler's dream.

Relationship Realities

Up-Close and Personal

If you're interested, a road relationship is great. Getting close with someone in a faraway place has a sense of excitement and mystery about it. The romantic whirlwind can seem freer and easier because you won't necessarily be held accountable for your actions. Perhaps you're into the good time now and then plan to move on. You're being independent. The folks at home don't need to know. This may make you feel more daring.

The downside is that humans everywhere are still human. People can misunderstand intentions and build up hopes, only to get hurt no matter what. Along with joy, travel can bring anxiety too. Be sure you want to add to the natural emotional ups and downs of travel by beginning a new relationship. Of course, if your friendship develops into sexual intimacy, be sure to use protection. Venereal disease and AIDS are a problem everywhere, and for all ages. Abstinence is the only guaranteed safeguard. Failing that, take care and use protection.

Staying Healthy and Fit

Where to Work Out

Carrying your home and your possessions with you for months on end on your back is a great way to stay in shape. But you still can get flabby and winded. Eating light and healthfully helps, along with getting regular exercise like jogging, walking, swimming, and calisthenics. All around the

Working a little exercise into the day's adventure makes staying fit easy. Kerry preps for reef dive, Taveuni Island, Fiji.

world there are tennis courts, swimming pools, sports fields, golf courses, and gyms in or around schools and universities, activity centers, and at YMCAs or YWCAs. Many towns and cities have local pay-per-use public sport facilities that are open to travelers. These usually are mentioned in travel guides.

But it's so easy to skip working out when you're on an easy-going travel adventure. So unless you're a dedicated exerciser, you'll have to learn to trick yourself into staying fit.

Travel As Workout

Tie it into travel adventure, and exercise seems to come naturally. For example, after slowly snorkeling along the depths of the reef, head back very near shore (so as not to attract any sharks with your flailing) and do a few laps afterwards. Or take a bus to a sightseeing destination, but walk or jog back to your lodging when you're ready to leave. Carry a Frisbee for playing with while you wait at a crossroads for the bus or train to come. Rent bicycles for the day somewhere instead of scooters. Tell yourself to climb that bluff for the reward of taking a great photo of the valley below, instead of for the huffing workout.

And of course, you can improvise little ways of getting your heart rate up, like calisthenics on a sportsfield or walking up the stairs to your room instead of taking the elevator.

Your body's a machine. Keep it tuned, and stay fit, and you'll require less sleep but still have more energy for the demands of active travel.

Gestures and Behavior

Body Language

Humans move and gesture in radically different ways around the globe. Below are some examples of the diversity.

In some parts of Asia, an up and down good-bye wave actually means "come here." A playful pat on the head of a person in Thailand is a serious personal affront. You should crouch lower than local elders in traditional Polynesia. In the Middle East, scratching your wrist resembles the crude, bold Arab taunt that's flashed in anger. The West's firm handshake is replaced by a firm grabbing of the testicles in part of the Trobriand Islands and in New Guinea. In some places you both receive items and eat with your right hand, as the left is traditionally reserved for toilet matters.

> While traveling in a Muslim country, a single friend traveling solo on trains and buses learned to discourage curious males by not just saying she was married, but by saying her husband was meeting her at the station. Other tips: wear a gold band, or carry pictures of children and say they're yours.

But most of the time you'll know what and what not to do. Your travel books should have some tips, but don't get overly concerned about these issues. Watch locals for clues, and just try to be respectful. Get ready for people to edge very close to you as they talk, because the concept of personal space has different perimeters wherever you go.

If you do unknowingly commit a faux-pas, and I'm sure I've done it a lot, usually you will be silently forgiven without being aware you did it at all. For detailed information on behaviors and customs in most of the world's countries, send for a CulturGram on a specific country. Write: Publication Services, Brigham Young University, P.O. Box 24538, Provo, UT 84602, (800) 528-6279.

Ethics and Your Impact

Traveling Responsibly

Travel is rich in delights. But no matter how nice or understanding a person you are, simply leaving your home and traveling to other parts of the world and bringing yourself and your gear and attitudes to areas not regularly visited is an intrusion into someone else's reality. No matter how careful you are, there's not much you can do about the fact that you're an interloper. So if you're going to travel, you have to be cognizant of your impacts as a human being and as a product of twentieth-century technology. The crew of *Star Trek's* Enterprise calls it observing the prime directive: not to interfere with alien cultures. We shouldn't either.

Let me illustrate this idea with a hypothetical example of a chance meeting.

Say you're off somewhere in a remote village in a developing country. You're with a couple of other travelers, and as you round a corner on the way to your lodging, you run into a group of kids playing with a soccer ball. They've recently moved to town so their father can find work, and they've had little contact with Westerners except maybe Rambo or James Bond in the movies.

A seven-year-old youth growing up in that poor, rural agricultural area in modest conditions doesn't necessarily see things from the same perspective as you. There's no TV, these kids don't read much if at all, the picture books at school—if there are any—are dated and reference nothing modern like big cities, skyscrapers, jets, and so on. The kids are blissfully ignorant and happy as clams.

But suddenly their eyes go wide. Before them is an apparition of three creatures cruising by their doorstep. These things look like humans, but they're wearing bandannas and strange accessories like shiny mirrored sunglasses and big black glinting cameras. One is listening to a Walkman with headphones on, and the woman in the trio has short shorts and a

Most cultures speak some English. If you don't speak their language, a smile and a few gestures will get you far. Maasai women, Kenya.

tank top on. They're all in spendy hiking boots, with big, rubbery, heavy-duty watches on their wrists. Their chic backpacks have bright, shiny, colored accents like lime green and dayglo purple and blaze red swatches all over them.

One of the travelers holds up his palm and attempts to give a "high-five"—a cultural slight here because it happens to be a gesture of aggression and not friendship—and then starts offering coins because the kids aren't coming closer. Another starts photographing the scene without asking, unaware that these locals happen to believe being photographed captures one's soul and removes it via film.

The woman asks in an unintelligible language where the homestay is. Met by silence, she holds out her guidebook and starts jabbing a finger at the description the kids can't read—though she assumes they should try and that it's their responsibility to know where the place is anyway.

There is nothing malicious in the travelers' actions. Yet it's quite a load for these innocent brains to process. The resources that allow these travelers to be there, with all their fine accoutrements, is likely out of the reach of these kids in their lifetime. It certainly is a jarring experience, though one with which the kids eventually may become familiar.

The more exposed people become to things they can't have, the more they may pine for them, leading to a sense of futility. They may develop feelings of shame, doubt, or embarrassment at their own cultural circumstances, which previously had been perfectly beautiful.

Ethically speaking, what right do you have to set other people's worlds upside down, whether you mean to or not? Circumstances of good fortune give some people—you, in this case—the opportunity to explore areas and cultures with which others are totally unfamiliar. It's exciting. It's neither right or wrong. It just is.

But we aren't granted the right to abuse our opportunities. Respecting others as you go can begin to heal ingrained resentment over misdeeds committed by other intruders in earlier months, years, and centuries.

Think on both the micro and macro level and you'll be a better traveler. Even something as simple as promising to send someone a photo you've taken of them and then not doing it can shade their opinion of outsiders for a lifetime. The fewer bad legacies we create, the better off we'll all be.

I wouldn't be offering a socially responsible travel discourse except that I once learned first-hand. On the first bright morning of my first remote tropical trip, I was sitting at a backpacker's hostel, recovering from a twelve-hour overnight flight and chatting with one of the native women kitchen helpers, who was sitting on the bench next to me on a break. I noticed right off the bat she was a very warm and friendly person. She lit a smoke, and threw the match in an attractive old antique tin that served as the ashtray.

I knew nothing of her language, but she spoke broken English, so I started making conversation. I picked up the dented ashtray and eyed it closely, then mentioned that where I come from it would be considered a valuable tin. I said I collected old antique tins, loved the graphics and old designs and colors, had maybe forty at home, often paid fifteen to twenty dollars for a good one, and was very proud of my collection.

In a jet lag haze I continued to drone forth, pointing out that while the ashtray was a coffee tin, I tended to collect tobacco tins. They were smaller and had more compact designs, with great detail in the lettering and graphics. I owned not just any tins, but a special set of vintage tobacco tins. Oh they were swell, I said, and boy did I plan to keep my eyes open to buy good ones on this trip!

Her big brown eyes looked into mine after this monologue, and with complete innocence she asked, "Why?"

> A friend and his sister were strolling around an Israeli market. A local with romance on his mind ambled over with the deal of the day: "This camel I got? Trade you my camel for your sister." Uh, no thanks but geez, thanks for the compliment!

Well, I'm sure I sputtered something. But that one word completely knocked me flat. My earnest attempt at sharing was a classic exercise in ignorance. I learned shortly thereafter that this woman's culture was one of unrestricted giving. Material things have little value, acquisition is frowned upon, working for money is considered destructive to the soul, and the more one can give away the better. The best way to live is to provide others—including uninvited travelers—all the food and hospitality one can muster, even at the expense of one's own meals. Being only recently familiar with my culture's preoccupation with gain, she saw my urge to collect and own things as ludicrous. I had assumed we were on the same wavelength because we were speaking the same language. That experience taught me a lot and I'm still reeling from it.

Coming Home

11

Aboriginals in Australia hunted kangaroos with boomerangs. Not the air kind, but larger ones they threw that bounced along the ground.

▲▼▲▼▲▼▲▼▲▼▲▼▲▼▲▼▲▼▲▼▲▼▲▼▲

Though clipper ships could supply England with dried Asian fruit, Queen Victoria offered a lordship to anyone who could deliver a fresh mangosteen.

▲▼▲▼▲▼▲▼▲▼▲▼▲▼▲▼▲▼▲▼▲▼▲▼▲

The Mayans distilled honey and licorice into a liqueur called Xtabentun. It's still made for sale in the Yucatan.

Has it been a month already? Three months? A year? Time has flown, and your foreign adventure is, alas, ending. The best part about coming back is knowing you can leave again. Whether you return to a clean slate or a full plate, you'll do fine. Here's more advice on getting through re-entry shock, adjusting to all the changes, making progress toward fitting back into the rhythms of home reality. It's time to be back with family and friends again. Time to work again. At least for long enough to rev up your plans for your next off-beat adventure, right?

The Last Day

The Return

You're at the airport, outside the capitol of a distant nation. Perhaps it's wild Botswana. Or exotic India. Or primitive Vanuatu. You sit at the gate and all your senses are heightened. It might not feel like good-bye, but an exit stamp is drying in your passport and your backpack's being loaded in the cargo hold of the plane. You close your eyes, and the waiting continues.

The crackle of a foreign voice echoes over the speakers and jars you. Boarding has started. This can't be the end, but it is. You rise, feeling light. An official in blue glances at you, then waves you on.

It feels like you're watching the final scene of a movie and starring in it at the same time. You watch as your hand comes up and pushes the door open onto the black tarmac, and you feel the tropical heat encase you. A hot wind brushes your cheeks. You squint, and cross toward the silver jet that's jiggling in the mirage of the rising heat. Sparkling sunlight bounces off the cabin.

You clutch the rail, climb the stairs, turn for a final look back at the airport, and then duck out of the hot breeze into the darker calm of the cabin. You find your seat and buckle in.

The gnawing of excitement in your stomach begins as the jet revs up, thunders down the runway and forces you back in your seat as it powers up, up, up to the skies. The plane levels. You made it. You're on your way. You begin to feel a release. You find yourself staring down out of the little window at the bright land way below, that moments ago was enveloping you. You didn't sleep much last night. What are these sad and happy feelings all about?

Coming home after a long time away brings mixed emotions. You're proud of yourself for having pulled off the trip. You have so much to tell others it could fill a book. And you're feeling the pangs of regret, not wanting to leave all the beautiful places and people you've seen and met.

Along with the emotions of leaving and returning, there's a sense of wonder. What did I achieve on this adventure? How do I make sense of what I've done? Was it as great as I expected? As you wing your way back home, it's starting to dawn on you. Home is returning to you, but you may not be ready to return to it. Time has passed, you moved forward, yet you're heading backwards.

Re-entry Shock

Reality is beckoning, and you may as well resign yourself to the fact that it will take some time to get used to it. It's commonly called culture shock or re-entry shock, and you'd better get ready, because home will seem as foreign as some of the places you've traveled to.

If you've been gone a long time, the apprehension first hits a couple of weeks before you depart. You've arranged how you're getting home, and lined up the last adventurous events of your trip. Suddenly, reality hits. Butterflies tickle your stomach, making it difficult to eat. You tell them to go away. Your body is preparing you for the shock of going back. It knows, and your mind is beginning to accept that you're going to have to deal with what you left behind and make home fit in with what you've learned abroad.

For us, the first time we experienced return culture shock it started with the gridwork of city streets. Stop signs. Street lights. Tall buildings. I did errands around the area the first few days at home, yet I couldn't roam. I felt channeled, held up, directed, squared, compressed, stopped, and frozen by traffic systems. I was used to

Sometimes, home is not where you thought. A friend was traveling in Egypt, came across a movie set, and got hired as an extra. The money was good, so he made the desert his new home for a month. In another instance, a friend came home after six months, found home old hat, and has since moved to the country she was last in.

It's normal to miss family and home, and yet want to travel further. The only sure antidote: keep your passport current. Grass airstrip, Venezuela.

being a rolling tumbleweed. I got anxious at stoplights. I had to go, man! But I couldn't, and had to adjust to the rhythms and systems of home life. The trip was over.

We gave in to the inexorable norms of being stateside. We didn't own a home, so we retrieved our car and rented a place to live. Got a phone number. Hired a moving van. Took stuff out of storage. Developed our slides and pictures. Got together with friends and family and exchanged gifts. Tried to find out what had happened in the region over the past year. Unpacked all the stuff we'd shipped. Plugged in the stereo, the TV, and set the alarm clock. Fired up the newspaper subscription. Prepared our résumés. And it wasn't long before we got jobs.

It's exciting to be home. You get to see family and friends again, and swap stories. But though you may be happy to be home, most people soon feel the undeniable urge to leave again. You're a veteran now, and you know how easy it is to pull off the kind of adventures this book is all about.

In my case, after coming back from that first long-term adventure I dug in my heels. I wouldn't cut my ponytail. Instead of tossing T-shirts from far-off lands in the laundry, I carefully handwashed them and hung them on hangers. Our pictures and souvenirs cluttered beds, shelves, floors, tabletops. As for our stories, I would hunt down listeners—store clerks were easy prey, captive at their registers—and launch into some overseas episode until I got cut off with "paper or plastic?" At get-togethers with friends or relatives I held forth, recounting this and that to patient ears, long after coffee cups were empty and the "can we go now?" body hints had started. I rigged up our mosquito net over the bed, trying to recreate "A Palace In The East."

Re-entry Encounters

There's also getting used to having all your belongings with you again. Living simply on the road lets you learn to live with less. Coming back to the "everything all the time" approach to Western life, where many people pursue consumption for its own end, can be unsettling. You'll find yourself going mute in the middle of conversations about making more money, buying new gadgets, wearing cool new fashion, investing in the stock market.

There's the shock of the commercial environment, the sheer bounty and efficiency of America. For example, there are the fully stocked, twenty-four hour mega-supermarkets with a profusion of cheese, meats, fruits, and vegetables, ten brands of ice cream, thirteen types of laundry detergent, thirty-six flavors of cereal, and whole aisles dedicated to pet food. The buses run on schedule. Someone in a four-wheel-drive vehicle crowds you from behind, talking into a cellular phone. There's hourly news, city traffic, omni-commerce, helicopters in the air, and lots of people. You're hearing the hum of the most modern nation, and it will take some time to get back into the clip of things.

Minimizing Shock

So here's a yardstick. For every month away, give yourself a month to feel comfortable about being home. After six or more months away or even up to a couple of years, six months transition is about what it takes. One guy told me his friend spent three years overseas in remote areas, came home, and couldn't handle the sudden encounters with doors, stairs, television, car repair, dry cleaners, or phone installation. It was too unnatural. He swears on a stack of bibles that his friend dug a cave in his backyard, moved in, then shifted to camping in a tent until he felt readjusted enough to live back inside. I doubt this happens often, but you never know. That's one of the wonders of travel.

Adapting to Changes

So where do you fit in, and how do you move on? Well, you go slow. If

> A face from home?
> A friend and his
> fiancee exited the
> Budapest, Hungary
> train station, and
> met a couple from
> Scotland. The Scottish
> pair looked vaguely
> familiar. It turns
> out the friend had
> waited on them at
> a restaurant and
> they'd chatted about
> music, back home
> in Washington State,
> three years prior.

you're in re-entry shock, you're still distressed merchandise. You won't want to commit yourself to things too quickly. You go with the decisions that feel right, and jettison dated behaviors and useless things. You get back on top of your financial situation, and reacquaint yourself with your career. Or perhaps start a new one.

After you get back into some basic organized patterns, deeper issues will start to surface. A few months home will show that you definitely have changed. A lot of the ideas you grew up with almost unconsciously will be reaffirmed or reconsidered. Your decision to leave and travel on a way-off adventure opened up a Pandora's box, and you're paying the price. This is part of the total travel experience. Your mind has to sift through your new knowledge and all the fresh ideas and feelings you gained on the trip.

Ongoing Benefits

Though you've returned from off-beat adventuring, the rewards continue. You may well find you're more confident of your place in the world, having experienced some of the rest of it. You've conquered certain places, so to speak, and rightly may feel a little glorious. You'll have learned so much about traveling by doing it that you'll savor it forever, or use it as a reason to depart again. You'll find you have a better inside knowledge of why other cultures act the way they do. Exotic behaviors and rituals make sense. You'll be able to get together with foreign people you meet or seek out in your home area as a way of staying connected to your memories.

And don't forget you'll be getting all those cool red and blue airmail letters in your mail from the foreign friends you made!

Making New Plans

We keep from going bananas by having pictures to look at and memories to sift through. We came home safely from the last trip and got on with life at home just fine. We also keep ourselves going by deciding to save our money instead of spending it. Travel has become a regular part of our life, and when we get enough saved we'll break away again for another incredible adventure of extended foreign travel. This time, we might dare to go for even longer.

See you on the horizon.

I would rather be ashes than dust—

I would rather

that my spark should burn out in a brilliant blaze

than it should be stifled by dryrot.

I would rather be a superb meteor,

every atom of me in magnificent glow,

than a sleepy and permanent planet.

The proper function of Man is to live, not to exist.

I shall not waste my days in trying to prolong them.

I shall use my time.

—Jack London (1876–1916)

Appendix 12

Painted lines were a confusing idea on Middle East roads. Reports tell of drivers assuming the center line was for straddling.

s▼▲▼▲▼▲▼▲▼▲▼▲▼▲▼▲▼▲▼▲▼▲▼▲▼▲

Test bootleg cassette tapes. Sometimes only half of each song appears, in attempts to fit whole albums on one side.

▲▼▲▼▲▼▲▼▲▼▲▼▲▼▲▼▲▼▲▼▲▼▲▼▲▼▲

In Malaysia, candied centipedes are a treat and packages of dried, chewy octopus chunks go by the name "The Chinese Chewing Gum!"

Packing List

Basic Gear List

- Backpack or large shoulder duffel
- Daypack
- Lock and cable
- Two or three little brass locks
- Down sleeping bag (cool climates and up to 70 degrees)
- Two single cotton sheets sewn together, rolled and stuffed in plastic trash sack (warm climates over 70 degrees and tropical)
- Two bungee cords to secure bag or sheets to backpack
- Nylon poncho
- Cotton walking shorts
- Cotton dress slacks or dress skirt
- Cotton dress shirt (button or polo) or dress blouse
- Light cotton sweater
- Two t-shirts
- River sandals or thongs
- Swiss army knife with tweezers
- Cotton bandanna
- Cotton bath towel
- Travel alarm or watch with alarm
- Camera and film
- Sima® or other thin lead bag for holding film
- Small, light flashlight (such as Maglight®) with two backup batteries and backup bulb
- Waist or body pouch for passport and money
- Ziploc baggies for storing papers
- Two pair underwear

- Two pair white cotton socks
- Two pair thin wool socks
- All-around washable sport shoe or light trail shoe/hiker
- Swimsuit
- Sunglasses with neck string
- Cotton sunhat
- Sturdy plastic sack (or extra nylon stuff sack) for soiled or wet clothes
- Small plastic bottle of clothes-washing detergent
- Small calculator (solar)
- Noise earplugs

Additional for Campers

- Waterproof tent (Gore-Tex™ or with waterproofed rain-fly and seams) with shockcord poles
- Thin plastic groundcloth
- Spool of nylon twine (often called parachute cord)
- Quart plastic water bottle
- Single gas cooking burner
- Kitchen gear in plastic pack
- Foam or self-inflating sleeping pad
- Biofilter drinking straw or pump water purifier (remote areas only)
- Matches

Other Basics to Consider, Depending on Location, Interests, and Activities

- Pair light hiking boots
- Whistle
- Swimfins, snorkel, mask (plastic lens; less weight)
- Lap swimming goggles
- Light Walkman and headphones

- Video camera
- Tripod
- Inflatable, sealable, waterproof camera bag
- Microcassette dictaphone
- Laptop computer
- Global positioning system (hand-held)
- Compass
- Paperback book(s)
- Battery-operated beard trimmer
- Art supplies
- Business cards or personal cards
- Mosquito repellent with Toluamide (DEET)
- Mosquito net and kite string (to hold net)
- Condoms, diaphragm, and jelly
- Pen and notepad
- Hammock
- Light, sturdy, collapsible umbrella
- Plastic cylinder with cap that hangs from neck, for keeping cash or travelers checks dry while swimming
- Inflatable neck pillow
- Small games, deck of cards

Basic Toiletries

- Nylon crushable toilet kit bag
- Toothbrush, small tube toothpaste, and dental floss
- Small bar soap in plastic container
- Small plastic bottle of shampoo, conditioner
- Plastic hand razor with extra blades and shave cream
- Nail clippers
- Plastic comb or brush

- Large, flat sink plug
- Small mirror

Women

- Two bras
- Minimal inexpensive jewelry
- First month's menstrual supplies
- Minimal cosmetics
- Pepper or mace spray

Special Items for Cold Climates

- Cotton or polypropylene top and long johns
- Insulated hiking or mountain boots
- Wool hat
- Wool gloves/ski gloves
- Fleece shell
- Extra pair wool socks
- Down or fiberfill jacket, either waterproof Gore-Tex™ or water-resistant

First Aid Medical Kit

- Aspirin
- Pain pills, like Tylenol with codeine
- Ibuprofen
- Small tube of antibacterial cream
- Acetaminephin
- Small tube of antifungal cream (with tolnaftate or chlortrimazole)
- Prescription antibiotics for infections
- Iodine
- Bandaids
- Ace-style bandage
- Hydrocortizone cream

- Pure aloe vera gel to soothe sunburn
- Pepto-bismal tablets
- Small folding scissors
- Lip sunscreen with zinc oxide
- Blister pads
- Vitamins
- Small bottle Lomotil
- Gauze
- Flu or cold pills
- Adhesive tape
- Snakebite kit (optional)
- Motion sickness pills or "the patch"
- Hand/face wipes in little tearpackets
- Prescribed pill medicines as indicated for regional disease (such as malaria pills) or for health condition (penicillin, special antibiotics, thyroid pills, etc.)
- Medic alert bracelet if needed

Gifts to Give to Locals

- Little lapel pins, earrings, or miniature charms from your home state
- Postcards of your town or state
- Pictures of your family (very popular)
- Sew-on patches or stickers of your state
- Paper beer coasters with a town tavern on it
- Slides of sights in your area to show or give away

Official Items and Papers

- Passport
- Credit Card
- U.S. Money
- Vaccination certificate

- International driver's license
- U.S driver's license
- Visas
- Charge card
- ATM card
- Traveler's checks
- Student ID card from high school, college, or university
- Teacher's ID card
- Youth Hostel Card
- Student discount card
- Photocopies of everything in a separate baggie
- Airline or other tickets
- Address book

Suggested Reading and References

Chapter 1

- Riley, Jack *Designing Quality And Balance Into Your Life, Work And Play*. Berkeley, CA: Wilderness Press, 1990.

- Peck, M. Scott. *The Road Less Traveled.*

- Robin, Vicki and Dominguez, Joe. *Your Money Or Your Life.* 1993.

- Reader, John. *Man On Earth, A Celebration Of Mankind: Portraits Of Human Culture In A Multitude Of Environments.* New York, NY: Harper & Row, 1990.

- Johnson O'Conner Research Foundation, 11 E. 62nd Street, New York, NY 10021. (212) 838-0550. Aptitude and interest testing & analysis service, with regional centers.

- *Life/Work Design Program*, Crystal-Barkley Corporation. (800) 346-8007. Software program guides user through career and lifestyle choices.

Chapter 2

- Cotlow, Lewis. *In Search Of The Primitive*. Boston, MA: Little, Brown & Company, 1966.

Chapter 3

- Wheeler, Maureen. *Travel With Children*. Berkeley, CA: Lonely Planet Publications, 1992.

- Jefferey, Nan. *Adventuring With Children*. Marston Mills, MA: Avalon House, 1990.

- Let's Take The Kids, 300 West Glenoaks Boulevard, Suite 201, Glendale, CA 91202. Travel club for families.

- Sygall, Susan and Lewis, Cindy. *A World Of Options For The 90s: A Guide To International Educational Exchange, Community Service, and Travel For Persons With Disabilities*. Eugene, OR: Mobility International, 1993.

- Shrout, Richard. *Resource Directory For The Disabled*. New York, NY: Facts On File, 1993.

- Society For Advancement of Travel For The Handicapped, 347 Fifth Avenue, Suite 610, New York, NY 10016. Organization with quarterly newsletter.

- *Specialty Travel Index*. 305 San Anselmo Avenue, Suite 217, San Anselmo, CA 94960. Special-interest travel list.

Chapter 4

- Malott, Gene and Adele. *Get Up And Go: A Guide For The Mature Traveler*. San Francisco, CA: Gateway Books, 1989.

- *Magellan's Essentials For The Traveler*. (800) 962-4943. Travel supplies catalogue.

- *Travel Matters*. Moon Publications, P.O. Box 3040, Chico, CA 95927. Newsletter on alternative travel.

- *Out And About*. (800) 929-2268. Gay and lesbian resort travel newsletter.

- *Traveler's Tales*. O'Reilly & Associates, 103A Morris Street, Sebastopol, CA 95472. Series of travel writings from recent country visitors.

- Zapatos, Thalia. *A Journey Of One's Own: Uncommon Advice For The Woman Traveler*. Portland, OR: Eighth Mountain Press, 1993.

- *Unique & Exotic Travel Reporter*, P.O. Box 1859, Bend, OR 97709. Newsletter of unusual travel trips.

- Axtell, Roger and Healy, John. *Dos And Taboos Of Preparing For Your Trip Abroad*. New York, NY: John Wiley & Sons, 1994.

Chapter 5

- *Commodores Bulletin*, Seven Seas Cruising Association, P.O. Box 1256, Stuart, FL 34995. Yacht information.

- *Free & Footloose*, Air Courier Association, 191 University Boulevard, Suite 300, Denver, CO 80206. (800) 822-0888. Courier newsletter.

- Field, Mark. *The Courier Air Travel Handbook*. Phoenix, AZ: Thunderbird Press, 1994.

- International Association of Air Travel Couriers, (407) 582-8320. Organization with newsletter.

- Discount Travel International, (212) 362-3636. Air courier screening and booking service, for budget-conscious travelers.

- Airhitch, (212) 864-2000. Matching service for travelers ready to go on low-cost, last-minute flights.

- Makower, Joel. *Every Kind Of Map And Chart On Earth And Even Some Above It*. New York, NY: Vintage Press, 1986.

- *Your Trip Abroad; Travel Tips For Senior Citizens; A Safe Trip Abroad; Tips For Americans Residing Abroad; Travel Tips For Older Americans; Country Background Notes*. Superintendent of Documents, USGPO, Washington, DC 20402. Helpful publications from the U.S. Department of State, Bureau of Consular Affairs.

- *Visa Requirements Of Foreign Governments*. Passport Services Branch, Room 386, 1425 "K" Street Northwest, Washington, DC 20524.

- *Freighter Travel News*, The Freighter Travel Club of America, 3524 Harts Lake Road, Roy, WA 98580. Newsletter.

- *Freighter Space Advisory*, (818) 449-3106. Bulletin from a freighter travel firm.

Chapter 6

- Bynum, Robert and Mazuski, Paula. *Manston's Before You Leave On Your Vacation*. Sacramento, CA: Travel Keys, 1989.

- Wade, Betsy. *The Practical Traveler's A-Z Guide*. New York, NY: New York Times Books, 1994.

- *How Safe Is Flying?* Air Transport Association, 1301 Pennsylvania Avenue Northwest, Washington, DC 20004. Trade group booklet.

- *Fly Rights*. U.S. Department of Transportation, 400 Seventh Street Southwest, Washington, DC 20590. Booklet.

- *Traveling With Your Credit Card*. BankCard Holders of America, 560 Herndon Parkway, Suite 120, Herndon, VA 22070. Booklet of tips.

- Forsyth, Stephen. *Defeating Jet Lag*. P.O. Box 2975, Shawnee Mission, KS 66201. Free pamphlet with a self-addressed, stamped envelope.

- *Going Abroad: 101 Tips For Mature Travelers*, Grand Circle Travel, 347 Congress Street, Boston, MA 02210. (800) 221-3610. Free brochure.

Chapter 7

- *Transitions Abroad*, P.O. Box 344, Amherst, MA 01004. Magazines and directories for overseas opportunities in travel, work, study, teaching, and volunteering.

- Graham, Scott. *Backpacking and Camping In The Developing World*. Berkeley, CA: Wilderness Press, 1989.

- *International Living*, 824 East Baltimore Street, Baltimore, MD 21202. Newsletter of overseas study, work, housing, and retirement, with annual ratings of quality of life in 160 countries.

- Endicott, M. L. *Vagabond Globetrotting*. Cullowhee, NC: Enchiridion Internation, 1989.

- Kohls, Robert. *Survival Kit For Overseas Living*. Yarmouth, ME: Intercultural Press, 1984.

- *YMCA/YWCA Worldwide Directory*, Y's Way International, 356 West 34th Street, New York, NY 10001.

- *Communities Directory*, Sirius Educational Materials, Baker Road, Shutesbury, MA 01072. Lists intentional communities and cooperatives worldwide.

- *The U.S. And Worldwide Travel Accomodations Guide*, Campus Travel Service, P.O. Box 5007, Laguna Beach, CA 92652. Lists school campus lodging.

- *Crisis Abroad: What The State Department Does; U.S. Consuls Help Americans Abroad.* U.S. Department of State, CA/P, Room 5807, Washington, DC 20520. Helpful booklets.

- Bezruschka, Stephen. *The Pocket Doctor.* Seattle, WA: The Mountaineers Books, 1992.

- Schroeder, Dirk. *Staying Healthy While Traveling In Asia, Latin America, And Africa.* Chico, CA: Moon Publications, 1993.

- Dessery, Brad and Robin, Marc. *The Medical Guide For Third World Travelers.* San Diego: KWP Publications, 1991.

- *Health Information for International Travel,* Superintendent of Documents, USGPO, P.O. Box 371954, Pittsburgh, PA 15250.

Chapter 8

- *Global Network Navigator Travel Center.* (800) 998-9938. Service for current worldwide travel information, via the Internet.

- Traveler's Remail Association, 6110 Pleasant Ridge, Arlington, TX 76016. (817) 478-9466. Mail holding and forwarding service.

- Traveler's Overnight Mail Association, Box 2010, Sparks, NV 89432. Mail holding and forwarding service.

- Wanderer's Worldwide Mail Service, 1916 Pike Place, Seattle, WA 98101. Mail holding and forwarding service.

- The Calvert School, 105 Tuscany Road, Baltimore, MD 21210. Grades K-8 correspondence school.

- The American School, 850 East 58th Street, Chicago, IL 60637. Grades 9-12 correspondence school.

- *ISS Directory of Overseas Schools.* Princeton, NJ: Petersen's Guides, 1990. (800) 338-3282. Lists schools abroad that teach children in English, with U.S. textbooks.

Chapter 9

- DuBois, Jennifer; Gutmann, Steve; Canfield, Clarke. *Now Hiring! Jobs In Asia.* Seattle, WA: Perpetual Press, 1994.

- Terry, Max. *Volunteer! The Comprehensive Guide To Voluntary Service In The U.S. And Abroad.* New York, NY: 1993.

- Griffith, Susan. *Work Your Way Around The World.* Princeton, NJ: Petersen's Guides, 1991.

■ *Work, Study, Travel Abroad: The Whole World Handbook.* New York, NY: St. Martin's Press for Council On International Educational Exchange, 205 East 42nd Street, New York, NY 10017. (800) 349-2433.

■ Willing Workers On Organic Farms, Mount Murrindal Co-op, Buchan, Victoria 3885, Australia. One of several WWOOF offices that places volunteers on farms worldwide.

■ Field Work Opportunities Bulletin, Archaeological Institute of America, 675 Commonwealth Avenue, Boston, MA 02215.

■ Vounteers For Peace, VFP International Work Camps, Tiffany Road, Belmont, VT 05730.

■ *The International Employment Hotline*, P.O. Box 3030, Oakton, VA 22124. Newsletter.

■ *REI Adventures' Travel Catalog 1994*, (800) 622-2236. Catalogue of all-inclusive adventure vacations from reputable firm.

■ The Adventure Center, (800) 227-8747. Four-wheel-drive overland odysseys up to 27 weeks, worldwide.

■ Simmons, James. *The Big Book Of Adventure Travel.* New York, NY: Plume, 1990. Adventure trip companies described and rated.

■ Muir-Bennett, Alison and Davis, Clare. *Hitch Hiker's Guide To The Oceans.* Stuart, FL: Seven Seas Press, 1990.

■ Patagonia, Inc.'s Guideline, (800) 523-9597. Service advises which adventure firms go where.

Chapter 10

■ Axtell, Roger. *Dos And Taboos Around The World: A Guide To International Behavior.* New York, NY: John Wiley & Sons, 1993.

■ Adventure Travel Society, 6551 South Revere Parkway, Suite 160, Englewood, CO 80111. Promotes sustainable travel.

■ Ecotourism Society, P.O. Box 755, North Bennington, VT 05257. Monitors environmental tourism.

■ The Nature Conservancy, 1815 Lynn Street, Arlington, VA 22209.

- Rainforest Action Network, 301 Broadway, Suite A, San Francisco, CA 94133.

- Habitat For Humanity, Habitat and Church Streets, Americus, GA 31709.

- Greenpeace, P.O Box 3720, Washington, DC 20007.

- World Wildlife Fund, 1250 Twenty-Fourth Street Northwest, Washington, DC 20037.

- Amnesty International, 322 Eighth Avenue, New York, NY 10001.

- Cultural Survival, 11 Divinity Avenue, Cambridge, MA 02138.

Chapter 11

- *Traveler's Tips on Bringing Food, Plant, and Animal Products into the United States.* U.S. Department of Agriculture, Inspection Service, Federal Center Building, Hyattsville, MD 20782.

- *GSP and the Traveler.* U.S. Customs Service, P.O. Box 7407, Washington, DC 20007. Booklet explaining the General System Of Preferences, which allows imports from certain countries to enjoy reduced or eliminated duty.

Share Your Experience...

Please complete this survey—detailing your extended vacation—and receive a twenty-five percent discount off the purchase of any Perpetual Press title when bought directly through Perpetual Press. See the order form on the following page for more information.

Personal Profile

Name: _____

Address: _____

City: _____

State: _____Zip: _____

Age: _____   Gender: Male   Female

College student?   Yes   No   Graduated?   Yes   No

Where did you hear about this book? _____
_____

What newspapers or magazines do you read regularly? _____
_____

Travel

Tell us your travel experiences to date. Places, best moments, advice, and tips. Attach a separate page if desired. _____
_____
_____
_____
_____
_____
_____
_____
_____
_____
_____
_____
_____
_____
_____
_____
_____
_____
_____
_____
_____

What did it cost? _____
_____
_____

General information

Positive aspects of this book: _____

_____

_____

_____

_____

Negative aspects of this book: _____

_____

_____

_____

_____

What should be added or changed: _____

_____

_____

_____

_____

Other comments: _____

_____

_____

_____

_____

May we contact you for additional information?   Yes   No
May we quote you in future editions?   Yes   No

Send your completed survey to:

Perpetual Press
P.O. Box 45628
Seattle, WA 98145-0628

If ordering other Perpetual Press titles, please enclose completed survey, order form, and payment and you will receive twenty-five percent off your order.

Perpetual Press Titles

If you would like to order additional copies of Perpetual Press titles, fill out the order form below. Please include $3.00 postage and handling for the first book and $.75 for each additional copy.

Copies

_____	$9.95	The Global Adventurer's Handbook
_____	$17.95	Now Hiring! Jobs in Asia
_____	$17.95	Now Hiring! Outdoor Jobs
_____	$17.95	Now Hiring! Destination Resort Jobs
_____	$14.95	Now Hiring! Jobs in Eastern Europe
_____	$14.95	Now Hiring! Ski Resort Jobs

_____ Total copies

$ _____ Total amount
$ _____ Less 25% discount (if completed survey is enclosed)
$ _____ Postage and handling

$ _____ Total enclosed

Send check or money order with this form to:

Perpetual Press
P.O. Box 45628
Seattle, WA 98145-0628

Name: _____
Address: _____
City: _____
State: _____Zip: _____
Phone: _____

Note: All Perpetual Press titles are also available at bookstores throughout the U.S. and Canada.

About the Author

John Malarkey, 35, is a veteran of several off-beat travel trips to the Pacific, Mexico, Australia, Asia, Europe, and the Middle East. An adventure-seeking traveler drawn to far off places, he visits regions using the same methods he writes about.

John is a sixth-generation Pacific Northwest native who graduated from the University of Oregon. His first extended vacation—touring Greece with his parents and grandmother at age nine—included hanging onto this donkey as it carried him up the crescent-shaped caldera island of Santorini.

This is his first book.